The New Novello Choral Edition

MENDELSSOHN

Elijah

An Oratorio for soprano, alto, tenor
and bass soli, SATB, orchestra and organ

Opus 70

Text derived from the Lutheran Bible by Julius Schubring
English version by William Bartholomew

Edited by
MICHAEL PILKINGTON

Vocal Score
(Mit deutschem Text und Vorwort)

Order No: NOV 070201

NOVELLO PUBLISHING LIMITED

CONTENTS
INHALT

FIRST PART
ERSTE THEIL

iii

NB   The layout of bars and page numbers in The New Novello Choral Edition corresponds exactly to that in Novello's previous edition, for ease of reference in rehearsal when both may be in use.

PREFACE

HISTORY

The first reference to the possibility of composing an oratorio on the subject of Elijah occurs in a letter written by Mendelssohn to his friend Karl Klingemann, who was helping to arrange a performance of *St Paul* in Liverpool. Dated 12 August 1836 it includes the sentence: 'If only you would give all the care and thought you now bestow upon "St Paul" to an "Elijah", or a "St Peter", or even an "Og of Bashan".'[1] On 18 February 1837 Mendelssohn again wrote to Klingemann: 'What I would like best would be for you to take "Elijah" − divide the story into two or three parts, write it out in choruses and airs, either in verse or prose of your own; or, compile it from the Psalms and Prophets, with powerful big choruses, and then send it to me. . . . You may let it be dramatic like "Judas Maccabaeus", or epic, or both combined'.[1] In the autumn of 1837 Mendelssohn came to England for the Birmingham Festival, and stayed with Klingemann. The two men spent some time working on a sketch for an oratorio on Elijah, which was then left for Klingemann to complete. However, by the spring of 1838 nothing further had been done, and the sketch was returned to Mendelssohn.

In the autumn of 1838 Mendelssohn enlisted the help of his friend the Revd Julius Schubring. On 31 October Schubring sent a plan of Part 1 to Mendelssohn, together with comments which include: 'I have sought throughout − although it is not always possible − to introduce pieces, not merely suitable to the particular situation in question, but such as might awaken an echo in the hearts of the hearers.'[2] The next day he wrote in more detail, including '. . . the thing is becoming too objective − an interesting, even a thrilling picture, but far from edifying the heart of the listener. . . . Therefore you must carefully consider whether this time you prefer to turn away from Church music (i.e. music which refreshes, consoles) and create a tone-picture after the manner of the "Blocksberg-Cantata" [Walpurgis Night]. If not, we must diligently set to work to keep down the dramatic, and raise the sacred element, and always aim at this.'[2] Mendelssohn's reply on 2 November has valuable indications of the way his mind was working: 'I figured to myself Elijah as a thorough prophet, such as we might again require in our own day − energetic and zealous, but also stern, wrathful, and gloomy; a striking contrast to the court rabble and popular rabble − in fact, in opposition to the whole world, and yet borne on angel's wings − − − I am glad to learn you are searching out the always heart-affecting sense of the Scriptural words; but if I might make one observation, it is that I would fain see the dramatic element more prominent, as well as more exuberant and defined − appeal and rejoinder, question and answer, sudden interruptions, etc., etc.'[3] In view of the problems Mendelssohn had later with the widow scene (No. 8) the following from the same letter is of interest: 'The omission of the passage of the widow, and also of the raven, is decidedly most advisable; and also the abridgement of the whole commencement, in order that the main points may be dwelt on to one's heart's content.'[3] On 17 November Schubring sent a draft of Part 2, but was clearly worried by Mendelssohn's remarks: 'I am more and more convinced that you will have to supply the principal part of the text yourself. How is one to know what is running through your mind on this or that occasion?' Mendelssohn's reply (6 December) restated his own position even more strongly: 'With regard to the dramatic element, there still seems to be a diversity of opinion between us. With a subject like "Elijah" it appears to me that the dramatic element should predominate, as it should in all Old Testament subjects, Moses, perhaps, excepted. The personages should act and speak as if they were living beings − for heaven's sake let them not be a musical picture, but a real world, such as you find in every chapter of the Old Testament; and the contemplative and pathetic element, which you desire, ought to be entirely conveyed to our understanding by the words and mood of the acting personages.' There is no further letter from Schubring on Elijah till February 1839, and in this he makes it clear that the subject, at least on Mendelssohn's terms, is too much for him. Nothing more was done for six years.

On 11 June 1845 the Birmingham Festival committee passed the following resolution: 'That it appears to this Committee desirable that the services of Dr Mendelssohn be obtained to act as conductor at the next Festival; and that he be requested to consider whether he can provide a new oratorio, or other music, for the occasion.' (Mendelssohn had attended previous Festivals in 1837, with *St Paul*, and in 1840 with the *Hymn of Praise*). On 24 July Mendelssohn replied with a provisional acceptance, adding: 'Since some time I have begun an oratorio, and hope I shall be able to bring it out for the first time at your Festival; but it is still a mere beginning, and I cannot yet give you any promise as to my finishing it in time.'[4] On 19 October Mendelssohn wrote again to the Birmingham Committee: 'The principal point about which I am uncertain is whether I shall be able to have my new oratorio ready in time for your Festival. There would have been no doubt of it, had I been able to continue my work quietly at Frankfort, as I began it. But now there are so many businesses here, at Dresden, and at Berlin, which took up all my leisure time during the last months, that I have not been able to go on with it. If the businesses continue as they have been (which, however, I hope they will not), I *shall not* be able to finish my oratorio in time. If they do *not* continue, I *shall* finish it in time.'[4] A story told by Madame Sainton-Dolby (who sang in the first performance of the revised version of *Elijah*) gives an idea of the state of the work at this time. Attending a dinner in Leipzig, where she was to perform on 25 October 1845, she sat next to Mendelssohn, who arrived late.

'He excused himself by saying he had been very busy with his oratorio; and then turning to me he said, "I have sketched the bass part, and now for the contralto." "Oh!" I exclaimed, "do tell me what that will be like, because I am specially interested in that part." "Never fear," he answered, "it will suit you very well, for it is a true woman's part – half an angel, half a devil." I did not know whether to take that as a compliment, but we had a good laugh over it.'[5]

On 16 December 1845, Mendelssohn sent a draft libretto to Schubring with a plea for assistance. (Lady Wallace's translation dates this 1842, but Edwards notes this as an error). His letter seems to imply a movement towards Schubring's desire for more edification and less drama, and concludes: 'The second part, moreover, especially towards the end, is still in a very unfinished condition. I have not as yet got a final chorus: what would you advise it to be?'[3] Schubring contributed a number of suggestions, and proposed that 'the overture, picturing a famine, must represent a period of three years.'[2] Mendelssohn's letter to Schubring of 23 May 1846, only three months before the first performance, shows a continuing dissatisfaction with Part 2, though 'I have now quite finished the first part, and six or eight numbers of the second are already written down. In various places, however, in the second part I require a choice of really fine Scriptural passages, and I do beg of you to send them to me! I set off tonight for the Rhine, so there is no hurry about them; but in three weeks I return here, and then I purpose forthwith to take up the work and complete it.'[3] Part I had in fact been sent to England the same day. The letter to Schubring continues: 'Now, however, the second part begins with the words of the Queen, "So let the Gods do to me and more also", &c. (1 Kings xix: 2); and the next words about which I feel secure are those in the scene in the wilderness (same chapter, 4th and following verses); but between these I want, *first*, something more particularly characteristic of the persecution of the prophet; for example, I should like to have a couple of choruses *against* him to describe the people in their fickleness and their rising in opposition to him; *secondly*, a representation of the third verse of the same passage; for instance, a duet with the boy, who might use the words of Ruth, "Where thou goest, I will go," &c. But what is Elijah to say before and after this? and what could the chorus say? Can you furnish me with, first, a duet and also a chorus in this sense? Then, until verse 15, all is in order; but there a passage is wanted for Elijah, something to this effect: "Lord, as Thou wilt, be it unto me" (this is not in the Bible, I believe?); for I wish that *after* the manifestation of the Lord, he should announce his entire submission, and after all this despondency declare himself to be utterly resigned and eager to do his duty. I am in want, too, of some words for him to say at, or before, or even after, his ascension, and also some words for the chorus. The chorus sing the ascension historically with the words from 2 Kings ii: 11, but then there ought to be a couple of very solemn choruses. "God is gone up with a shout" (Psalm xlvii: 5) will not do, for it is not the Lord but Elijah who went up; however,

something of *that* sort. At the close, I should wish to hear Elijah's voice once more. . . . Lastly, the passages you have sent for the close of the whole (especially the trio between Peter, John and James) are too historical and too far removed from the grouping of the (Old Testament) story; I could, however, manage to get over this difficulty by composing a chorus, instead of a trio to these words. It can easily be done, and I think that I shall probably do it.'[3] Schubring's reply a week later was clearly helpful, though he is still convinced 'the oratorio can have no other than a New Testament ending. Elijah must help to transform the old into the new covenant – that gives him his great historical importance.'[2]

F.G. Edwards quotes from a number of letters showing how hard Mendelssohn was working in the spring of 1846: to Hauser of Vienna – 'I sit, over both my ears, in my "Elijah", and if it turns out only half as good as I often think it will, I shall be glad indeed! The first part will be quite finished within the next few days, and a goodly portion of the second part also. I like nothing more than to spend the whole day in writing the notes down, and I often come so late to dinner that the children come to my room to fetch me, and drag me out by main force.'[5] To Jenny Lind – 'I am getting a little confused, through writing down, during the last few weeks, the immense number of notes that I previously had in my head, and working them now and then upon the paper into a piece, though not quite in the proper order, one after another.'[6] To his sister Fanny – 'I am more driven than ever, as an immense piece of "Elijah" is not yet copied, whilst the first part is already in rehearsal in England. . . . The first thing tomorrow morning I shall shut myself up, and decline to budge till "Elijah" is finished, which may not be for another three weeks, and that also I swear by my beard.'[7]

The following letter, written by Mendelssohn to Moscheles (Conductor-in-chief of the Festival) is worth quoting for the light it throws on the character of the composer. 26 June 1846: 'My dear Friend, – The occasion of these lines is a passage in Mr Moore's letter, in which he says: "Nearly the whole of the Philharmonic band are engaged [for Birmingham]; a few only are left out who made themselves unpleasant when you were there." [At a Philharmonic rehearsal in 1844]. Now, I strongly object to this restriction; and as I fancy you can exercise your authority in the matter, I address my protest to you, and beg you to communicate it to Mr Moore. There is nothing I hate more than the reviving of bygone disputes; it is bad enough that they should have occurred. This one of the Philharmonic is, so far as I am concerned, dead and buried, and must on no account have any influence on the selection made for the Birmingham Festival. If men are to be rejected because they are incompetent, that is not my business and I have nothing to say in the matter; but if it is because "they made themselves unpleasant when I was there", I consider that an injustice, against which I protest. Any further disturbance on the part of these gentlemen, I am sure, is not to be feared. That at least is my belief, shared probably by all concerned. So you will sincerely oblige me by having the selection made exactly as if I were not coming to England. The only consideration that can be shown me is not to take me into consideration at all. You will do me a favour by putting this very strongly to Mr Moore, and requesting him to let the matter drop. If my wishes are to be complied with, the incident must herewith end. Should it be otherwise, I shall write a dozen letters in protest against what I should consider a spirit of vindictiveness. Excuse all this. Ever yours, Felix.'[3,8] (Joseph Moore was manager of the Birmingham Festivals).

On 23 June William Bartholomew (see **The Translation**, below) was able to write to Mendelssohn to say the choruses of Part 1 'will this day be in the hands of the engravers.'[9] They must have worked remarkably quickly, since according to Edwards 'It was not until after the middle of June, only two months before the Festival, that Mr Stimpson (the chorus master) received the first instalment of the chorus parts. Although these were printed (all the rest of the oratorio was sung and played from MS copies), the deciphering of them was no easy matter, owing to the many alterations – black, red and blue ink being freely used to indicate the alterations and re-alterations in the parts.' Many of these alterations must in fact have been made after Bartholomew had received Mendelssohn's letter of 3 July, his first list of detailed comments on the translation of Part 1. 'As late as 3 August, twenty-three days before the performance, the arrival of the first two choruses of Part 2 was reported, and the last chorus was not received till nine days before the Festival!'

The first performance took place on the morning of 26 August 1846 in Birmingham Town Hall, conducted by the composer. It was an immense success, though the soprano, Madame Caradori-Allen, caused Mendelssohn some problems. At the first rehearsal (with piano, in London, on 19 August) she asked him to transpose 'Hear ye, Israel' down a tone (it was composed with Jenny Lind in mind) and make other alterations, for 'it was not a lady's song'! Mendelssohn settled this by threatening to engage another singer (Madame Caradori's fee was to be the same as Mendelssohn's own!). On 20 and 21 August orchestral rehearsals were held at the Hanover Square Rooms. (The parts had been tried over and corrected in Leipzig.) There was a full rehearsal in Birmingham Town Hall on Monday 24 August. According to the *Birmingham Journal* 'After the oratorio had been rehearsed, Mendelssohn expressed himself highly pleased with the manner in which the performers had rendered his work, and complimented them on their extraordinary efficiency.' However, 'At Mendelssohn's request the usual Tuesday evening concert was given up for an extra rehearsal of "Elijah".' (Edwards). The performance was on a large scale: an orchestra of 125, 93 strings and doubled woodwind; 79 sopranos, 60 altos (all male), 60 tenors and 72 basses. The principal soloists were Madame Caradori-Allen, Miss Maria B. Hawes, Mr. Charles Lockey, and Herr Staudigl. Although James Stimpson, the chorus master, was official organist for the Festival Dr Henry Gauntlett

was specially engaged to play the organ in *Elijah*.

After the performance *The Times* wrote: 'The last note of "Elijah" was drowned in a long-continued unanimous volley of plaudits, vociferous and deafening. It was as though enthusiasm, long-checked, had suddenly burst its bonds and filled the air with shouts of exultation. Mendelssohn, evidently overpowered, bowed his acknowledgements, and quickly descended from his position on the conductor's rostrum; but he was compelled to appear again, amidst renewed cheers and huzzas. Never was there a more complete triumph – never a more thorough and speedy recognition of a great work of art.' Mendelssohn's own comments in a letter to a friend (Frau Livia Frege of Leipzig) after the performance form a valuable guide to his aims in this work and in general: the soprano part 'was all so pretty, so pleasing, so elegant, at the same time so flat, so heartless, so unintelligent, so soulless, that the music acquired a sort of amiable expression about which I could go mad even today when I think of it. The alto had not enough voice to fill the hall. . . . but her rendering was musical and intelligent, which to me makes it far more easy to put up with than want of voice. Nothing is so unpleasant to my taste as such cold, heartless coquetry in music. It is so unmusical in itself, and yet it is often made the basis of singing and playing – making music, in fact.'[3,6]

Immediately after the performance Mendelssohn started work on the piano arrangement, and during the following months much of the work was revised. A letter to Klingemann of 6 December 1846, includes: 'I have again begun to work with all my might at my "Elijah", and hope to amend the greater part of what I thought deficient at the first performance. . . . I shall most seriously revise all that I did not deem satisfactory; and I hope to see the whole completely finished within a few weeks, so as to be able to set to work on something new. The parts that I have already remodelled prove to me again that I am right not to rest till such work is as good as it is in my power to make it; even though very few people care to hear about such things, or notice them, and even though they take very much time; yet the impression such passages, if really better, produce in themselves and on the whole work, is such a different one, that I feel I cannot leave them as they now stand.'[1] Mendelssohn's sincerity in these remarks is shown by the fact that in this very letter he writes: 'I have quite completed one of the most difficult parts (the Widow)', and yet on 8 February writes to Bartholomew: 'I am going to send a *new song* for the Widow', and Bartholomew's translation is not returned to Mendelssohn till 3 March! (For details of the revisions see under **The Translation** below).

In the spring of 1847 Mendelssohn returned to England to conduct the first performances of the revised oratorio. Six performances were given in 15 days, starting at Exeter Hall in London on 16 April. On 20 April he conducted a performance by the Hargreaves Choral Society in the Free Trade Hall, Manchester. He returned to London for an *Elijah* on the 23rd and an orchestral concert on the 26th.

He then went to Birmingham for another *Elijah*, for the benefit of James Stimpson, for which he asked no fee or expenses. This was in spite of the fact that he had yet more London *Elijah* performances on the 28th, and 30th. This placed an enormous burden on the composer's fragile health. On his return home he learnt of the death of his sister Fanny, at only 41. The strain was too great, and though a holiday in Scotland seemed to be of help, he died on 4 November 1847.

The first performance in Germany took place in Hamburg on 9 October 1847, conducted by August Krebs (1804-1880). Mendelssohn himself was due to conduct *Elijah* at performances on 3 November in Berlin and on 14 November in Vienna, the latter with Jenny Lind singing for the first time the part the composer had written for her. But Mendelssohn cancelled his Berlin appearance even before a severe stroke partially paralysed him on 1 November. The performance went ahead, nevertheless, conducted by Julius Schneider, while the Vienna performance, brought forward to 12 November and conducted by the chorus-master, Schmidl, became a memorial concert with all the participants in mourning clothes and Mendelssohn's empty rostrum draped in black with a scroll of music and a laurel wreath on the desk.

From contemporary pictures it would appear that neither the Singakademie in Berlin nor the hall of the Musikverein in Vienna were large enough to accommodate the size of forces used in Birmingham or London. Indeed, there would appear to be a significant difference between the influence of *Elijah* in England and its reception in German-speaking countries. Whereas in England the work seems to have been a major catalyst in the growth in the number and size of choral societies, in the composer's homeland the oratorio appears to have achieved little success. The first Leipzig presentation, conducted by the composer's long-term associate, Julius Rietz (1812-77), in the Gewandhaus, marked the beginning of the decline in Mendelssohn's popularity in Germany, a decline encouraged in no small part by the anti-semitic views of Wagner and his followers. The Gewandhaus was half empty, the audience response apathetic.

In contrast, a year after Mendelssohn's death, a 'grand performance of the Oratorio of *Elijah*, in aid of the "Mendelssohn Foundation for Free Scholarships in the Leipzig Musical Conservatory" ' (according to *The Times*, 16 December 1848), took place in the Exeter Hall. It was organised by Jenny Lind and sold out. Lind not only took part herself but also encouraged others to donate their services, and was a leading figure in setting up the Mendelssohn Scholarship Fund, the first beneficiary (in 1856) being Arthur Sullivan.

Mendelssohn's own financial reward was 250 guineas from Edward Buxton of Ewer and Ewer for the English copyright of *Elijah*. Then, after the composer's death, Buxton sent a further 100 guineas, unsolicited, to Mendelssohn's widow. (350 guineas was reckoned to be the equivalent, in 1963, of 30,000 DM.) The score published in June 1847 by Ewer sold for 36 shillings; the first octavo edition (1852) cost 10 shillings and was an immediate best-seller.

THE TRANSLATION

The libretto of Elijah was written in German, based on the Lutheran Bible. Since the work was designed for performance in England a translation was needed. Mendelssohn asked William Bartholomew (1793-1867), who had already translated many of his other works, to provide this. Mendelssohn supervised the work in great detail by letter, in English, for both the original and revised versions. All comments relating to the latter are given below. It is clear the two men had great respect for each other's abilities.

Rather than quote from the letters in the order in which they were written the numbers of the oratorio are taken in order, with such comments as may be relevant. (M = from Mendelssohn to Bartholomew[9]; B = from Bartholomew to Mendelssohn.[10] The letter from Mendelssohn of 3.7.46* is reproduced in facsimile in F.G. Edwards, and some of Bartholomew's marginal comments are given here).

*All dates are given in the form day. month. year.

FIRST PART
Introduction Designed from an early stage to be the opening of the oratorio. 'I wish to keep this if possible as in the English Bible version; therefore I propose:-'   (M 3.7.46)

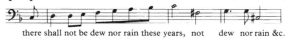

there shall not be dew nor rain these years, not   dew nor rain &c.

Overture 'I hope you will have time to write an overture, or introduction, unless you expressly design there shall be none.' (B 23.6.46). 'My intention was to write no Overture, but to begin directly with the curse. I thought it so energetic. But I will certainly think of what you say about an Introduction, although I am afraid it would be a difficult task, and do not know what it should or could mean before that curse. And after it (I first thought to write the Overture *after* it), the chorus *must* immediately come in.' (M 3.7.46). In a later letter Bartholomew wrote: 'I have maturely considered, and, with Mr K[lingemann], think it will be a new feature, and a fine one, to announce the curse, No. 1. Then let an introductory movement be played, expressive, descriptive of the misery of famine – for the chorus (I always thought) comes so very quickly and suddenly after the curse, that there seems to elapse no time to produce its results.' After quoting this letter F.G. Edwards writes: 'It seems evident that Mendelssohn was indebted to Bartholomew for the suggestion of an overture to "Elijah".' But note Schubring, in January 1846, 'The overture, picturing a famine, must represent a period of three years.'

No 1 Much changed for 1847.

No 3 The English version of the first sentence has caused some problems. All the original editions have the line as printed in the main body of this score, with no punctuation after 'garments' and a colon or semicolon after 'transgressions'. This is retained in the recent Eulenberg study score, though Julius Rietz has commas after both words. The alternative version in this score appears in the Novello vocal score of 1885 and has the advantage of making sense, and matching the German. Novello 1903 uses the revised words, but with the original punctuation, thus rendering the sentence almost meaningless.

No 4 'The time is *Andante tranquillo*. The first words are from Jer. xxix: 13. And the following from Job xxiii: 3, and I wish to keep these last literally: "Oh, that I knew (*slurred*) where I might find Him, that (added note, as you also have) I might come even to His seat" (or "presence", perhaps, if the two notes shall not be slurred)'. Bartholomew had: "Ah! could I find Him; and at His footstool bow before His presence." 'And before the first subject and the first words return, the notes may be altered thus:-'

(M 3.7.46)

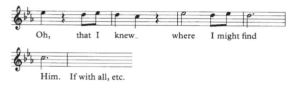

No 6 Rewritten for 1847.

No 7 'Pray let the beginning stand as in the Bible, viz:-

and if the end "and thus harm thee" can be spared, and it can finish with the words "against a stone", I should like it better' (M 3.7.46). The end of this was altered for 1847. 'Recit. "Now Cherith's brook", bar 9. I do not quite like *your two* slurs at the end; and as you do not like *my* notation, what if we tried a third mode? viz:-

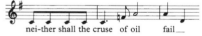

Now adopt which you like of the *three*.' (M 8.2.47).

No 8 This scene was entirely rewritten for 1847. 'In the 13 bars which I have added before the chorus "Blessed are the men" [No 9], and which are taken from Psalm cxvi [12] and Deut. vi: 5, I wrote the German words under the English in case you should prefer the notation as originally composed, and choose to add a word or a syllable here and there in the English version, in order to give it the same rhythm as in German. I should wish this in the passage just quoted, particularly in the beginning of Elijah's answer, "Du sollst den", where the two slurred notes "Thou ♩ shalt " are not equally good. But I could not find something else, and I also think that passages like this are best left as in the Bible' (M 30.12.46). 'I do not speak of bar 26 and bar 38 of No 8, because Mr Buxton will have informed you that I am going to send a *new song* for the Widow, and that therefore the whole No 8 must be postponed till then.... Bar 157 [page 46 bar 3], I do not

like the two Bs and two Cs on the words "render to the"; could it not be:-

or, if you object to this, it must be at least –

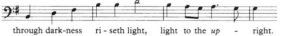

but I confess that I do *not like the quavers*, if they *can* be got rid of.' (M 8.2.47). 'I like all the passages of the translation you send me with but two exceptions. . . . in the new No 8 – the words from Psalm vi which you hesitate to adopt are, of course, out of the question; but I also object to the second part of the sentence which you propose to add to the words of Psalm xxxviii, viz.: "I water my couch" etc. – I do dislike this so very much, and it is so poetical in the German version. So if you could substitute something in which no "watering of the couch" occurred, but which gave the idea of the tears, of the night, of all that in its purity. Pray try!' (M 3.3.47)

The widow blames Elijah for her son's illness because the presence of a man of God automatically brings hidden sins to light, so that God can no longer overlook them, thus causing retribution.

No 9 Altered and rescored for 1847. 'Is it as scriptural to say "the men" as "the man"? ['Either way is objectionable' B]. And if not, could the sentence be "Blessed is the man who fears Him, who delights", and so on? And what do you like better: the amplification, "light shining over them", or to say instead of these words, "to the upright", and to slur the two notes thus:-

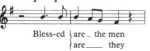

['This is better than "shining over them"' B]. Pray do it as *you* think best.' (M 3.7.46). 'In the following chorus, No 9, there is a curious specimen of the different *meaning* of the German and English version: the words "He is gracious", &c. (or, as you had it, "*they* are gracious"), apply, in your version, to the righteous, while in ours they apply to God, and the passage is in our version, "the light ariseth to the righteous *from* Him who is gracious, full of compassion", &c, &c. Now I certainly composed it with this last meaning, and the question is whether you would think it advisable to introduce it, or not. I proposed "He is" instead of "they are" because I thought it could then be understood both ways; but most probably you might hit on something much better still. Instead of "who delight in His commands" I preferred "they ever walk in the ways of peace" *only*, as more expressive, and I hope you will be of my opinion. I see in the Birmingham book that you quoted the words of this chorus [as] Psalm cvi: 3; but I took them from Psalm cxxviii: 1, and Psalm cxii: 1 and 4, although nearly the same passage occurs in Psalm cvi: 3.' (M 30.12.46). 'Bar 10: I cannot approve of the twice F in the soprano, although I quite acknowledge the truth of your observation. But I propose instead:-

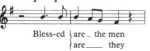

If you dislike this, pray propose another mode; but the soprano *cannot* have the two F while the tenor also has them. Bar 14 as *you* have it. Instead of your and my bar 13, I propose:-' (M 8.2.47)

men_____ who fear___ Him.

No 10 Some alterations for 1847. 'At the beginning I should wish to have the same words as in No 1, viz: "before whom I stand", instead of "I tell you truly". I prefer "Let him be God" to "He shall be God" (which you have added in pencil). Instead of "I, even I alone stand here among you", I propose the alteration:-

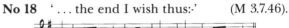
I, e - ven I, on - ly re - main,

I prefer "Invoke your forest gods", etc, as you do.' (M 3.7.46)

    Jezebel, wife of Ahab, was daughter of the king of Tyre in Phoenicia. The Phoenicians worshipped the nature god Melkart, known to the Israelites, as were all foreign nature gods, as Baal. When Jezebel married Ahab she brought her religion with its idols, priests and prophets with her.

No 11 'Is not the accent extírpate a wrong one? ['No' B]. The syllable *tir* will always be the first in the bar and the strongest, with a marked accent.' ['And it should be' B] (M 3.7.46).

No 12

'
Or he is per-su - ing.

and then –

jour - ney; or per-ad - venture

(M 3.7.46).

No 13 'Could not the words "with lancets cut yourselves after your manner" be kept?' (M 3.7.46).

No 14 Some alterations for 1847.

No 15 'A piece for which I must again require your friendly assistance. From the time I first sent it away for the Birmingham performance I felt it should not remain as it stood, with its *verses and rimes*, the only specimen of a Lutheran Chorale in this old-testamental work. I *wanted* to have the *colour* of a Chorale, and I felt I could not do *without it*, and yet I did not like to have a Chorale. At last I took those passages from the Psalms which best apply to the situation, and composed them in about the same style and colour, and very glad I was when I found (as I looked into the English Bible) that the beginning went word by word as in German. But after the beginning my joy was soon at an end, and there it is I must ask you to come to my assistance. The words are taken from Psalm lv: 23; Psalm cviii: 5; and Psalm xxv: 3.' (M 30.12.46). In 1846 the words

ran: 'Regard thy servant's prayer, / While angels bow before Thee, / And worlds around thy throne / In strains of praise adore Thee. / O, help him in his need, / Thy gracious ear accord – / Jehovah Sabaoth, / Creator, God, and Lord!' 'The music was also altered, but its quartet-chorale form and slender accompaniment were retained.' (Edwards).

No 16 Much altered for 1847. 'Could not the end be: "and we shall have no other god before Him", or "the Lord" (from Exodus xx: 3)? ['And we *will* have no other God but God the Lord' B]. Then instead of "let not a prophet" I propose:' (M 3.7.46).

and let not one of them es-cape ye;   *bring* them; &c

'I added the German words . . . in pencil, because I thought that the English translation, "adoring" etc., did not express the meaning entirely, nor did it render the rhythm of the German, which is still more to be felt by the bar I have added before the pause. Our "fallt nieder" means something still more awful, I think, than to "bow down" or "to adore", but query whether it can or should be given in English!' (M 30.12.46). In 1846 the words read: 'Bow down, bow down! on your faces fall adoring!'

No 18 ' . . . the end I wish thus:-' (M 3.7.46).

Woe un-to them,   woe___ un-to them.

No 19

'
                    O Lord, Thou hast o - ver

thrown thine en - e-mies, and des-troy'd them! Now

look on us, &c.

Then I wish the following notes altered:-

        Go up now, child, and look to-ward the

sea.   Has my prayer_ been heard by the Lord?

I also prefer "the heavens are *as* brass" – a note might be added. Then afterwards I propose:-

clo - sed up, *be - cause they have sinn'd*___

_ *have sin-ned a-gainst Thee*

And afterwards if "and turn from *their* sin" seems preferable to you, a note might be added to keep the words as in the Bible. In the following sentence it sounds to me more scriptural to leave the words as in 2 Chronicles vi: 27:-

Then hear from heav'n and for-give___ the sin,

Then I wish the notes altered thus:-

Go up a-gain, and still look to-wards the sea.

Then also "the earth is *as* iron." And then would you like this:-

There is a sound of a-bun-dance of rain.

['Altered, but not like this because if he hears a sound of rain in abundance he need not pray afterwards for the answer to his wish.' B. However, this is how the scene is presented in 1 Kings 18. It is also worth noting the following from Mendelssohn's letter to his brother Paul concerning the first performance: 'How often I thought of you during the time! More especially, however, when the "sound of abundance of rain!" came . . .'[3]]. If possible I should wish to have omitted "I implore Thee" which does not sound as scriptural to me. If I am wrong pray leave it; but if not, the words "to my prayer" might be repeated instead of them. The following is Psalm xxviii: 1:-

Un-to Thee will I cry, Lord, my

rock: be not si-lent to me.

and could not the following sentence be thus:-

\and Thy great mer - cies do re-mem-ber, O Lord!
or/Thy gra-cious

['Altered, not quite like this' B]. Then I prefer:-

like a man's hand!

Instead of "His boundless" I propose to omit the G (the first note), and have instead "for His" (mercies, &c.), and to add afterwards a note (A), in order to say "endureth *for* evermore".' (M 3.7.46).

No 20 'I prefer "The Lord is *above them*" to "is the highest".' (M 3.7.46).

SECOND PART

No 21 Added to and reconstructed for 1847. Part 2 originally opened with a tenor recitative, omitted for 1847. 'The Recit. which I now send is taken from Isaiah xlix: 7. Here again the English words went at first perfectly well, but afterwards they would not do at all, and (which is the most essential) their meaning differed greatly. The German means that the Lord speaks "to the soul that is despised and *to the nation* which is abhorred by others, and to His servant who is *oppressed by tyrants*", and all this made me adopt the words for this Recit., and therefore

I wish it to be expressed also in the English version.' (M 30.12.46). 'I prefer —

Who_ hath be-liev-ed our re-port

then:

-veal-ed to

It *must* be —

be not a-fraid, be

and not:

be not a -

which will not do for the quickness of the movement. Bar 89 is impossible as you propose, because on the a♯ and g♯, &c., *there must be no words* pronounced; they *must be* slurred notes, as in the German wording, and moreover they must be sung on a good syllable (no "u", or "o", or, &c.). So I should propose:-

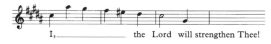

I,_____ the Lord will strengthen Thee!

And at any rate pray *let the notes be slurred*, because it is essential to the whole of the song. The same also when the passage is repeated, bar 140. Bar 148 must be so:-

for I thy

All those passages I do *not* mention here are quite excellent in the way you propose.' (M 25.2.47)

Mendelssohn was clearly concerned about the short recit. on page 111; the meaning he expresses above is made clear in the New English Bible: 'Thus says the Holy One, the Lord who ransoms Israel'. It might make this easier to understand if *and* were to be omitted, giving *his* the crotchet, as in the German. Though the first editions have no comma after 'Israel', showing how it was intended to be read, the rhythm makes it almost impossible to make this clear to the listener; the comma printed in Rietz and all subsequent editions confuses the sense.

No 22 'Yet still it shall not come nigh thee.' For 'it' see Psalm 91: 5,6.

No 23 Revised for 1847.
'The sins of Jereboam'. Some sixty years before Ahab came to the throne Jereboam became the first northern king of a divided Israel when the ten northern tribes rebelled against Solomon's son Reheboam. Judah was left with two tribes, but also with Jerusalem. Jereboam had to found other centres of worship, and set up golden calves to serve as symbols of the presence of Jehovah. Since the bull was the object of Canaanite worship (a nature god, therefore a Baal) this was the beginning of the invasion of foreign gods which received its first defeat at Mount Carmel. Jezebel's destruction of the prophets of Jehovah was a last attempt to save the

situation; it ended in failure. For the end of Jezebel see 2 Kings 9. See also 1 Kings 21 for the story of Naboth, killed by Ahab who wished to possess his vineyard.

No 24 New for 1847, the chorus which appeared at this point in 1846 being discarded.

No 25 New for 1847. The four instrumental bars at the end were an afterthought − Bartholomew had written − 'What if an interlude (short) gave time for the journey? and then, spent with fatigue, he might, from very weariness, say, "It is enough"'!!'

No 27 The words of the psalm as given in Simrock and the Ewer libretto are an exact quotation from the Authorised Version, and it was not thought necessary to change them in the Revised Version. The Prayer Book has 'The *angel* of the Lord tarrieth *round about* them that fear him'. Even the New English Bible has 'The *angel* of the Lord is on guard *round* those who fear him'. However, the Ewer version with its many angels has been followed by all subsequent editions, and the British Library copy of Simrock has been altered in pencil to match.

No 28 Originally a duet, with quite different music.

No 30 [Bar 30] ' "that Thou would'st please destroy me" sounds so odd to me − is it scriptural? If it is, I have no objection, but if not, pray substitute something else.' (M 3.3.47).

No 31 'In the song, "O rest in the Lord" (*Sei stille dem Herrn*), I beg you will adopt something like the words of Ps. 37, v.4, instead of the words "and He will ever keep the righteous"! "and He shall give thee" does very well with the notes; and there is only another expression, instead of "the desires of thy heart", necessary to make it fit the music and everything. And instead of the end "He will defend thee" &c., I should prefer also Ps. 37, v.8, perhaps so: "and cease from anger, and fret not thyself", or, "and cease from anger and forsake the wrath", which will do with the alteration of one or two notes being not slurred instead of slurred, and *vice versa*. And pray let always *accent* go first, especially in the *Choruses*! And Songs! And Recitatives!' (M 21.7.46). On 20 July 1846, crossing Mendelssohn's letter just quoted, Bartholomew wrote to Mendelssohn: 'Do you know a Scotch air, called "Robin Gray"?

Now compare the aria ... with it.' The original version ran thus:

He goes on to say he and two friends had all noted the similarity, and also quotes from the cadences.

Mendelssohn replied on 28 July: 'I do not recollect having heard the Scotch ballad to which you allude, . . . but as mine is a song to which I have always had an objection (of another kind), and as the ballad seems much known, and the likeness very striking, and before all, as you wish it, I shall leave it out altogether (I think) . . . Perhaps I shall bring another song in its stead, but I doubt it, and even believe it an improvement if it is left out.' Bartholomew replied 'Why omit the song "O rest", when merely a note or two of the melody being changed would completely obliterate the whole identity, and I think not spoil the song as a whole? If you omit it, and especially upon such a reason as my hint may have afforded, I shall be very much pained.' After further discussion this was done.

Note Mendelssohn's tempo − crotchet, not quaver, = 72.

No 33 'In the Recit. "Hear me speedily, O Lord", I have altered the beginning of the words thus:-

1 Kings xix: 9; Ps. xxii: 12, 20. Pray alter the English words accordingly, and look that the following alterations are made in the music of that same Recitative: bar 16 (accompaniment) is to be thus:-

Bar 22 (accompaniment) is to be thus:-

Bar 24 the voice is to be thus:-

and bar 27 (the last) is to be thus in the voice:-'

(M 2.2.47)

No 34 'I again wish to alter the notes in order to keep the English scriptural version. ... The beginning I wish altered thus:-

And be-hold, the Lord passed by.

or, if "passed" must have two syllables:-

Lord pass - ed

The end of the first phrase "as he approached" (bars 26 – 30) is not quite agreeable to me; could you not find *four* syllables instead of them (making the two *slurred* notes single ones) – e.g., "as the Lord drew near" (don't laugh), or something in which *the accent on the last syllable is strong and decided*! Then comes:-

But the Lord was not in the tem - pest.

Then again: "And behold the Lord passed by." And at the end again, "But the Lord was not in the earthquake." Also the third time: "But the Lord was not in the fire."

But the Lord, &c.

Then –

And af-ter the fire there came a still small voice

(here I think it is *quite* necessary to keep the scriptural expression *at least* at the beginning!). And then perhaps: "And in that voice the Lord came unto him." ' (M 18.7.46). 'I prefer:-

Be - hold, *God* the

and afterwards –

But *yet* the

and likewise –

But *yet* the

for I should not like to place the word "God" on so short a note, and in such a rhythm, while the word *yet* is just as light and insignificant as will do on such a note.' (M 26.9.46).

No 36   New for 1847.
'my glory': 'The noblest part of my being, the soul, heart, rational life; capable of praising God; parallel with soul.' (A.H. McNeile, in 'A New Commentary on Holy Scripture', ed. Gore, Goudge and Guillaume, SPCK 1928). This meaning does not appear in OED, but is clearly correct.

No 37   'I find the English words will apply literally to my music.' (M 10.8.46).

No 38   'I should prefer: "his words *appeared* like burning torches" – I am so obstinate about the *torches* because they account for the F minor character which I gave to that beginning more than any other word could possibly do.' (M 26.9.46). F.G. Edwards has a note: 'It is very difficult to fathom a composer's mind; but what *can* be the connection between "torches" and the key of F minor?'

Horeb and Sinai are alternative names for the same mountain, upon which Elijah met the Lord in Nos. 30—36 of the oratorio. This whole chorus is taken from a summary of the life of Elijah which occupies the first part of Chapter 48 in Ecclesiasticus. Changing the first word from 'Then' (which in the biblical context means: after the actions of Jereboam) to 'Thus' might make this clear. The German libretto is a direct quotation from the Lutheran bible, and has 'Und' not 'Dann'. The translation in the New English Bible is easier to understand: 'You heard a denunciation at Sinai, a sentence of doom at Horeb.'

No 40   It is worth noting that the tense of this quotation was changed for the oratorio. Malachi was prophecying the future return of Elijah, not describing his past actions, and wrote: 'Behold, I *will* send you Elijah'. Since the German also retains the future tense it might be justifiable to alter 'hath sent' to 'shall send'. 'He' in the second sentence refers to Elijah, not to the Lord.

No 41   'The *second* part of No 41, "Er wird öffnen die Augen der Blinden" must also be left out; so that from the words "und der Furcht des Herrn" [bars 52 – 3] it goes immediately to the quartet in B flat "Wohlan, denn".' (M 9.8.46). (This was an *alla breve* movement of 86 bars.) 'I decidedly prefer the *second* version of the beginning of No 41: "But the Lord from the north hath raised *one*!" (this is very good) but at the last bar before the *Andante* I cannot approve of.

instead of

Indeed these two long notes are *necessary*, for the development of the whole phrase, as I intended it. Now, could you not say "*call His name*", instead of "call upon His name"? Then the chief difficulty would be removed. And perhaps would it be possible to leave out "of the sun", and only say "from the rising" (this is done very often, at least in our German Bible)? Then the second passage would also stand nearly as with the German words:-

And from the ri - sing he shall call His Name

The rest of the *Andante con moto* suits my music now very well in the alteration, as you wrote it out, but I should prefer there the first, and in the beginning (*Andante sostenuto*) the second version. And why not? So the *Andante con moto* might begin: "But the Lord hath upraised one, the Lord," etc. But if this is against your conscience, leave here also the second version. For the beginning is much more important. I prefer:'

He shall   call   up - on His Name

[p.191, letter A]. (M 26.9.46). (For comment on the tempo marks see below under **Metronome Marks**). 'And I write over the Chorus "But, saith the Lord,

I have raised one", the German word "Schluss-Gesang" – *including this* Chorus, the following Quartett, and the last Chorus. Could you find an English word which might be applied as well? It must not be Finale, because that reminds me of an Opera; and it must not be "Final Chorus", because it shall mean Two Choruses and a Quartett; but I should like to have some word at the head of these three pieces, to show clearly my idea of their connection, and also as a kind of "Epilogue" contrasted with the "Prologue", or "Introduction" before the Overture.' (M 2.2.47).

The strange expression 'come on princes' means little without the rest of the verse; the Revised Standard Bible has 'he shall trample on rulers'. 'Trample' would fit the music better than 'come on', and be much more comprehensible.

On p.190, bars 6 and 7, Ewer gives the following alternative harmonies in the alto, tenor and piano parts.

Presumably this is an earlier version which remained uncorrected in the manuscript from which the Ewer edition was prepared.

No 42   Entirely rewritten to fresh words.

The anonymous editor of Novello 1903 takes pride in having altered the English words from 'ever shall reward you' to 'shall be thy rereward', on the grounds that this is more Biblical. The Authorised Version reads: 'and thy righteousness shall go before thee: the glory of the Lord shall be thy rereward.' The New English Bible makes the balancing of the two phrases clear: 'your own righteousness shall be your vanguard and the glory of the Lord your rearguard.' If the editor had used the spelling of the Revised Version – 'rearward' – it would have been clearer, but even so this second phrase makes little sense alone in English. The German has a slightly different meaning – 'the Lord will take charge of you' or 'guide you' – which can stand alone. It is also possible that Bartholomew (like many people since) thought of the word as re-reward rather than rere-ward, and felt he was merely clarifying rather than changing its meaning. The result is certainly nearer the German, and more easily fitted to the music. To confuse matters even further some recent printings of the 1903 edition have altered 'rereward to 'reward' in the introductory note, though leaving 'rereward' in the actual chorus!

METRONOME MARKS

F.G. Edwards provides a facsimile of a list of metronome marks received by Bartholomew from Mendelssohn on 9.4.47, for the first performance of the revised *Elijah* at Exeter Hall. There are a few disagreements with those finally printed:

No 10   Between the *Allegro vivace* (bar 14, renewed at **A** and at the top of page 56) and the *Maestoso* (7 bars before letter **C**) there is given an *Andante*, ♩ = 72, presumably at letter B.

No 30   The *Allegro vivace* and *Allegro moderato* are given simply as *Allegro* and *Moderato*.

No 32   ♩ = 60, not 66.

No 33   *Andante* ♩ = 76, not 72.

No 40/41   In Simrock the Recit. and Chorus form No 40, the Quartet being No 41; in Ewer the Recit. is No 40, the Chorus No 41, and the Quartet No 41a. It seems clear from Mendelssohn's letter of 26.9.46, quoted above, that the change from *Andante sostenuto* to *Andante con moto* should take place at bar 8 of the Chorus rather than at the beginning, as given in both scores.

EDITORIAL PROCEDURE

No autograph of the full score of the original version is known, though the copyist's version used at Birmingham, formerly in the Novello archive, was sold by the Granada Group at a Phillips auction in June 1989. An autograph vocal score is held in the Margaret Denecke Mendelssohn Collection at the Bodleian Library (GB-Ob-MDM C.39), extensively revised for the second version. The autograph of the revised full score is at Krakow (PL-Kj-Bd, 51). The full score was printed in 1847 by Simrock, with German and English words, and a vocal score with German words only. At the same time Ewer (subsequently taken over by Novello) printed the vocal score in a beautifully bound and printed folio volume, with English words only. This contained a short table of errata, corrected when this folio edition was reissued in 1850. There is also a Ewer octavo vocal score, in a more modern printing style, with both English and German, which the British Library catalogue also dates 1847, with a reissue in 1852. The copy is undated, and appears to be revised in places, particularly over punctuation. There is one major difference – the overture is given in a version for piano duet. It seems probable that this was in fact a somewhat later publication. Edwards states that an octavo edition 'did not appear till five years later' (1852). It has only been used here when there are disagreements between the other three sources.

These three editions, prepared under Mendelssohn's instructions, have been used as the basis of the present one. All discrepancies in the voice parts are shown. Where these relate to the underlay of the English it is usually taken that the English publication has priority, though there are a few cases where Simrock's full score is clearly to be preferred. Punctuation is not consistent, even in the German of the two Simrock scores. The vocal scores have been taken as a starting point; where markings are inconsistent, or appear to be missing, they have been added from the full score, with some help from Ewer 1852. No markings have been added unless they appear in one of the above sources. The accompaniment in the Simrock and Ewer vocal scores is virtually identical, hardly surprising, since this must be Mendelssohn's own arrangement; in the few cases of disagreement the full score has been used as the deciding factor. Simrock has rather more dynamic markings. In this edition dynamics and phrase markings in normal print appear in the piano scores and the full score; small dynamics and phrase marks with lines through appear in one or both the piano scores, but not in the full score; square brackets show markings from full score only. Metronome marks are given in the full score, Ewer 1852, and for the Second Part only, Ewer 1847; they agree throughout. In notes and ossia 'Simrock' refers to the full score; 'Simrock VS' to the German vocal score; 'Ewer' to the 1847 folio first edition, and 'Ewer 1852' to the octavo edition where this differs. The libretti are printed as in the original scores, apart from added biblical references. The Simrock full and vocal scores print the same (German only) libretto, and neither this nor Ewer's English libretto wholly matches the words as found in the music.

The most recent Novello vocal score was published in 1903, edited anonymously. It claims to agree with the full score edited by professor Julius Rietz as part of 'Mendelssohn Werke: Kritisch durchgesehene Ausgabe', published by Breitkopf und Härtel, 1874 – 77. However, it is clear that the latter was based solely on the full score, and that professor Rietz had a tendency to tidy up inconsistencies of phrasing without comment. Moreover, the 1903 edition has in many cases returned to the original German notes and rhythms, adapting the English underlay to fit, thus undoing Mendelssohn's careful work as detailed above. The accompaniment was also revised, incorporating more of the orchestral parts than Mendelssohn considered feasible for two hands.

Although there are 42 separate numbers in this work very few breaks should actually be made. 1 – 5 are continuous; so are 6 – 9, followed by 10 – 17. 18 seems to be intended as an interlude before 19 – 20 completes the First Part. 21 – 22 form the introduction to the Second Part, 23 – 29 are continuous, as are 30 – end, apart from a short pause between 39 and 40. A few other breaks are possible, but not to be recommended. It is clear that Mendelssohn's primary interest was in the dramatic effect of the work, and any unnecessary break weakens the drama.

Michael Pilkington, Old Coulsdon, 1991.

REFERENCES

Most of the information in this Preface comes from The History of Mendelssohn's Oratorio 'Elijah', by F.G. Edwards. Novello, Ewer and Co., 1896. This consists of 130 pages of information regarding the creation of *Elijah*, its first performance, and subsequent revision. Sources used by Edwards are listed below:

1. Letters to Karl Klingemann loaned by Dr Carl and Dr Felix Klingemann to F.G. Edwards and translated by him.

2. Briefwechsel zwischen Felix Mendelssohn Bartholdy und Julius Schubring, zugleich ein Beitrag zur Geschichte und Theorie des Oratoriums. Herausgegeben von Prof. Dr. Jul. Schubring, Direktor des Katharineums zu Lübeck. Leipzig: Verlag von Duncker und Humblot. 1892. English translations by F.G. Edwards.

3. Letters of Felix Mendelssohn Bartholdy from 1833 to 1847. Edited by Paul Mendelssohn Bartholdy and Dr Carl Mendelssohn Bartholdy, 1863. Translated by Lady Wallace. Longmans, Green and Co. 1863, new edition 1878. Though Edwards made acknowledgement to Longmans Green he revised Lady Wallace's occasionally clumsy translations, and these revisions are used here.

4. Letters to Joseph Moore, manager of the Birmingham Festival from 1802 to his death in 1851, written in English; loaned to F.G. Edwards by William Moore.

5. Quoted, as if told to himself, by F.G. Edwards.

6. Memoir of Madame Jenny Lind-Goldschmidt. H. Scott Holland and W.S. Rockstro. John Murray. 1891.

7. 'I tender my best thanks . . . to Mrs Victor Benecke (Mendelssohn's elder daughter), who has very kindly helped me to obtain permission to publish several letters relating to "Elijah" which have hitherto been unknown.' F.G. Edwards.

8. Letters of Mendelssohn to I. and C. Moscheles. Felix Moscheles. Trübner, Leipzig, 1888.

9. Miss Elizabeth Mounsey, sister-in-law of William Bartholomew, enabled F.G. Edwards to acquire the originals of fourteen letters written, all in English, by Mendelssohn to his translator.

10. 'I am greatly indebted to Frau Geheimrath Wach, of Leipzig (Mendelssohn's younger daughter), and her daughter, for their kindness in copying the long correspondence on "Elijah" from Bartholomew to Mendelssohn.' F.G. Edwards.

Libretto as printed in the Ewer edition, with biblical references as given by Bartholomew. Additional references, marked with an asterisk, are taken from Mendelssohn's letters. Those marked with a dagger have been added or corrected by the editor.

ELIJAH
AN ORATORIO

The Author of this English Version has endeavoured to render it as nearly in accordance with the Scriptural Texts as the Music to which it is adapted will admit: the references are therefore to be considered rather as authorities than quotations.

FIRST PART

INTRODUCTION (Bass)

Elijah As God the Lord of Israel liveth, before whom I stand, there shall not be dew nor rain these years, but according to my word. [1 Kings 17: 1]

OVERTURE

No 1 CHORUS

The People Help, Lord! wilt Thou quite destroy us? The harvest now is over, the summer days are gone, and yet no power cometh to help us! [Jeremiah 8: 20] Will then the Lord be no more God in Zion? [Jer. 8:19*]

RECITATIVE CHORUS

The deeps afford no water; and the rivers are exhausted! The suckling's tongue now cleaveth for thirst to his mouth: the infant children ask for bread, and there is no one breaketh it to feed them! [Lamentations 4:4]

No 2 DUET AND CHORUS

The People Lord, bow Thine ear to our prayer. [Psalm 86:1,6†]

Duet Zion spreadeth her hands for aid; and there is neither help nor comfort. [Lam. 1:17]

No 3 RECITATIVE (Tenor)

Obadiah Ye people, rend your hearts and not your garments for your transgressions; even as Elijah hath sealed the heavens through the word of God. I therefore say to ye, Forsake your idols, return to God: for He is slow to anger, and merciful, and kind and gracious, and repenteth Him of the evil. [Joel 2:12, 13]

No 4 AIR

Obadiah If with all your hearts ye truly seek me, ye shall ever surely find me. Thus saith our God. [Deuteronomy 4:29; Jer. 29:13*]

Oh! that I knew where I might find Him, that I might even come before his presence. [Job 23:3]

No 5 CHORUS

The People Yet doth the Lord see it not: He mocketh at us; His curse hath fallen down upon us; His wrath will pursue us, till He destroy us. [Dt. 28:15†; 28:22]

For He, the Lord our God, He is a jealous God; and He visiteth all the fathers' sins upon the children to the third and fourth generation of them that hate Him. His mercies on thousands fall – fall on all them that love Him and keep his commandments. [Exodus 20:5, 6]

No 6 RECITATIVE (Alto)

An Angel Elijah! get thee hence; depart and turn thee eastward: thither hide thee by Cherith's brook. There shalt thou drink its waters; and the Lord thy God hath commanded the ravens to feed thee there: so do according unto His word. [1 Kgs. 17:3-5†]

No 7 DOUBLE QUARTET

Angels For He shall give His angels charge over thee; that they shall protect thee in all the ways thou goest; that their hands shall uphold and guide thee, lest thou dash thy foot against a stone. [Ps. 91:11, 12]

RECITATIVE (Alto)

An Angel Now Cherith's brook is dried up, Elijah; arise and depart; and get thee to Zarephath; thither abide: for the Lord hath commanded a widow woman there to sustain thee. And the barrel of meal shall not waste, neither shall the cruse of oil fail, until the day that the Lord sendeth rain upon the earth. [1 Kgs. 17:7,9,14]

No 8 RECITATIVE AND AIR (Soprano)

The Widow What have I to do with thee, O man of God? art thou come to me, to call my sin unto remembrance? – to slay my son art thou come hither? [1 Kgs. 17:18] Help me, man of God! my son is sick! and his sickness is so sore, that there is no breath left in him! [1 Kgs. 17:17] I go mourning all the day long; [Ps. 38:6] I lie down and weep at night. [Ps. 6:6†] See mine affliction. [Job 10:15] Be thou the orphan's helper! [Ps. 10:14]

RECITATIVE

Elijah   Give me thy son. [1 Kgs. 17:19†] Turn unto her, O Lord my God; in mercy help this widow's son! For Thou art gracious, and full of compassion, and plenteous in mercy and truth. [Ps. 86:16,15] Lord my God, O let the spirit of this child return, that he again may live. [1 Kgs. 17:21]

The Widow   Wilt thou show wonders to the dead? Shall the dead arise and praise thee? [Ps. 88:10]

Elijah   Lord my God, O let the spirit of this child return, that he again may live!

The Widow   The Lord hath heard thy prayer, the soul of my son reviveth! [1 Kgs. 17:22]

Elijah   Now behold, thy son liveth! [1 Kgs. 17:23]

The Widow   Now by this I know that thou art a man of God, and that His word in thy mouth is the truth. [1 Kgs. 17:24] What shall I render to the Lord, for all his benefits to me? [Ps. 116:12*]

Both   Thou shalt love the Lord thy God; with all thy heart, and with all thy soul, and with all thy might. [Dt. 6:5*] O blessed are they who fear Him! [Ps. 128:1]

No 9 CHORUS

Blessed are the men who fear Him: they ever walk in the ways of peace. Through darkness riseth light to the upright. He is gracious, compassionate; He is righteous. [Ps. 112:1,4]

No 10 RECITATIVE AND CHORUS

Elijah   As God the Lord of Sabaoth liveth, before whom I stand; three years this day fulfilled, I will show myself unto Ahab; and the Lord will then send rain again upon the earth. [1 Kgs. 18:15,1]

Ahab   Art thou Elijah? he that troubleth Israel! [1 Kgs. 18:17†]

Chorus   Thou art Elijah, he that troubleth Israel!

Elijah   I never troubled Israel's peace: it is thou, Ahab, and all thy father's house. Ye have forsaken God's commands; and thou hast followed Baalim! [1 Kgs. 18:18]
Now send and gather to me, the whole of Israel unto Mount Carmel: there summon the prophets of Baal, and also the prophets of the groves, who are feasted at Jezebel's table. Then we shall see whose God is God the Lord. [1 Kgs. 18:19,21]

Chorus   And then we shall see whose God is the Lord.

Elijah   Rise then, ye priests of Baal: select and slay a bullock, and put no fire under

it: uplift your voices, and call the God ye worship: and I then will call on the Lord Jehovah: and the God who by fire shall answer, let him be God. [1 Kgs. 18:23,24]

Chorus   Yea; and the God who by fire shall answer, let him be God.

Elijah   Call first upon your God: your numbers are many: I, even I, only remain, one prophet of the Lord! Invoke your forest-gods and mountain deities. [1 Kgs. 18:22,† 25]

No 11 CHORUS

Priests of Baal   Baal, we cry to thee; hear and answer us! Heed the sacrifice we offer! hear us, O hear us, Baal! [1 Kgs. 18:26]
Hear, mighty god! Baal, O answer us! Let thy flames fall and extirpate the foe! O hear us, Baal!

No 12 RECITATIVE

Elijah   Call him louder; for he is a god! He talketh; or he is pursuing; or he is in a journey; or peradventure, he sleepeth; so awaken him: call him louder. [1 Kgs. 18:27]

CHORUS

Priests of Baal   Hear our cry, O Baal! now arise! wherefore slumber?

No 13 RECITATIVE

Elijah   Call him louder! he heareth not. With knives and lancets cut yourselves after your manner: leap upon the altar ye have made: call him, and prophesy! Not a voice will answer you; none will listen, none heed you. [1 Kgs. 18:28, 26, 29]

CHORUS

Priests of Baal   Hear and answer, Baal! Mark how the scorner derideth us! Hear and answer!

RECITATIVE

Elijah   Draw near, all ye people: come to me! [1 Kgs. 18:30]

No 14 AIR

Lord God of Abraham, Isaac, and Israel! this day let it be known that Thou art God; and I am Thy servant! O show to all this people that I have done these things according to Thy word! O hear me, Lord, and answer me; and show this people that Thou art Lord God; and let their hearts again be turned! [1 Kgs. 18:36, 37]

No 15 QUARTET

Angels   Cast thy burden upon the Lord, and He shall sustain thee. He never will suffer the righteous to fall: [Ps. 55:22] He is at thy right hand. [Ps. 16:8]
Thy mercy, Lord, is great; and far above the heavens. [Ps. 108:4†] Let none

be made ashamed that wait upon Thee! [Ps. 25:3]

No 16 RECITATIVE
Elijah   O Thou, who makest Thine angels spirits; – Thou, whose ministers are flaming fires; [Ps. 104:4] let them now descend!

CHORUS
The People   The fire descends from heaven; the flames consume his offering! Before Him upon your faces fall! The Lord is God: [1 Kgs. 18:38,39] O Israel, hear! Our God is one Lord: [Dt.6:4†] and we will have no other Gods before the Lord! [Dt. 5:7†]

RECITATIVE
Elijah   Take all the prophets of Baal; and let not one of them escape you: bring them down to Kishon's brook; and there let them be slain. [1 Kgs. 18:40]

CHORUS
The People   Take all the prophets of Baal; and let not one of them escape us: bring all, and slay them!

No 17 AIR
Elijah   Is not His word like a fire: and like a hammer that breaketh the rock in pieces? [Jer. 23:29]

For God is angry with the wicked every day: and if the wicked turn not, the Lord will whet His sword; and He hath bent His bow and made it ready. [Ps. 7:11,12]

No 18 AIR (Alto)
Woe unto them who forsake Him! destruction shall fall upon them, for they have transgressed against Him. Though they are by Him redeemed, yet they have spoken falsely against Him. [Hosea 7:13]

No 19 RECITATIVE AND CHORUS (Tenor)
Obadiah   O man of God, help thy people! Among the idols of the Gentiles, are there any that can command the rain, or cause the heavens to give their showers? The Lord our God alone can do these things. [Jer. 14:22]

Elijah   O Lord, Thou hast overthrown thine enemies and destroyed them. Look down on us from heaven, O Lord; regard the distress of Thy people: open the heavens and send us relief: help, help Thy servant now, O God! [2 Chronicles 6:27]

The People   Open the heavens and send us relief: help, help Thy servant now, O God!

Elijah   Go up now, child, and look toward the sea. Hath my prayer been heard by the Lord? [1 Kgs. 18:43]

The Youth   There is nothing. The heavens are as brass above me! [Dt. 28:23]

Elijah   When the heavens are closed up because they have sinned against Thee; yet if they pray and confess Thy name, and turn from their sin when Thou dost afflict them; then hear from heaven, and forgive the sin! Help, send Thy servant help, O God! [2 Chron. 6:26,27]

The People   Then hear from heaven, and forgive the sin! Help! send Thy servant help, O God!

Elijah   Go up again, and still look toward the sea. [1 Kgs. 18:43]

The Youth   There is nothing. The earth is as iron under me! [Dt. 28:23]

Elijah   Hearest thou no sound of rain? [1 Kgs. 18:41†] – seest thou nothing arise from the deep?

The Youth   No, there is nothing.

Elijah   Have respect unto the prayer of Thy servant, O Lord my God! [2 Chron. 6:19] Unto Thee will I cry, Lord, my rock; be not silent to me; [Ps. 28:1] and Thy great mercies remember, Lord!

The Youth   Behold, a little cloud ariseth now from the waters; it is like a man's hand! The heavens are black with clouds and with wind: the storm rusheth louder and louder! [1 Kgs. 18:44†,45]

The People   Thanks be to God for all His mercies! [Ps. 106:1]

Elijah   Thanks be to God, for He is gracious, and His mercy endureth for evermore! [Ps. 106:1]

No 20 CHORUS
Thanks be to God! He laveth the thirsty land! The waters gather; they rush along; they are lifting their voices! [Ps. 93:3]

The stormy billows are high; their fury is mighty. But the Lord is above them, and Almighty! [Ps. 93:4]

SECOND PART

No 21 AIR (Soprano)

Hear ye, Israel; hear what the Lord speaketh: – "Oh hadst thou heeded my commandments!" [Isaiah 48:1,18]

Who hath believed our report; to whom is the arm of the Lord revealed? [Isa. 53:1]

Thus saith the Lord, the Redeemer of Israel, and his Holy One, to him oppressed by tyrants: [Isa. 49:7] thus saith the Lord: – I am He that comforteth; be not afraid, for I am thy God, I will strengthen thee. [Isa. 41:10] Say, who art thou, that thou art afraid of a man that shall die; and forgettest the Lord thy Maker, who hath stretched forth the heavens, and laid the earth's foundations? [Isa. 51:12,13] Be not afraid, for I, thy God will strengthen thee.

No 22 CHORUS

Be not afraid, saith God the Lord. Be not afraid, thy help is near. God, the Lord thy God, saith unto thee, 'Be not afraid!' [Isa. 41:10]

Though thousands languish and fall beside thee, and tens of thousands around thee perish; yet still it shall not come nigh thee. [Ps. 91:7]

No 23 RECITATIVE AND CHORUS

Elijah   The Lord hath exalted thee from among the people: and over his people Israel hath made thee king. [1 Kgs. 14:7] But thou, Ahab, hast done evil to provoke him to anger above all that were before thee: [1 Kgs. 16:30†] as if it had been a light thing to walk in the sins of Jereboam. Thou hast made a grove and an altar to Baal, and served him and worshipped him. [1 Kgs. 16:31,32,33] Thou hast killed the righteous, and also taken possession. [1 Kgs. 21:19†]

And the Lord shall smite all Israel, as a reed is shaken in the water; and He shall give Israel up, and thou shalt know He is the Lord. [1 Kgs. 14:15,16†]

The Queen   Have ye not heard he hath prophesied against all Israel?

Chorus   We heard it with our ears. [Jer. 26:11]

The Queen   Hath he not prophesied also against the King of Israel?

Chorus   We heard it with our ears.

The Queen   And why hath he spoken in the name of the Lord? [Jer. 26:9]

Doth Ahab govern the kingdom of Israel while Elijah's power is greater than the king's? [1 Kgs. 21:7]

The gods do so to me, and more; if, by tomorrow about this time, I make not his life as the life of one of them whom he hath sacrificed at the Brook of Kishon! [1 Kgs. 19:2]

Chorus   He shall perish!

The Queen   Hath he not destroyed Baal's prophets?

Chorus   He shall perish!

The Queen   Yea, by the sword he destroyed them all!

Chorus   He destroyed them all!

The Queen   He also closed the heavens! [Ecclesiasticus 48:3†]

Chorus   He also closed the heavens!

The Queen   And called down a famine upon the land. [Ecclus. 48:2†]

Chorus   And called down a famine upon the land.

The Queen   So go ye forth and seize Elijah, for he is worthy to die; [Jer. 26:11] slaughter him! do unto him as he hath done!

No 24 CHORUS

Woe to him, he shall perish; for he closed the heavens! And why hath he spoken in the name of the Lord? Let the guilty prophet perish! He hath spoken falsely against our land and us, as we have heard with our ears. [Jer. 26:11] So go ye forth; seize on him! He shall die!

No 25 RECITATIVE

Obadiah   Man of God, now let my words be precious in thy sight. [2 Kgs. 1:13] Thus saith Jezebel: 'Elijah is worthy to die.' [Jer. 26:11] So the mighty gather against thee, [Ps. 59:3] and they have prepared a net for thy steps; [Ps. 57:6†] that they may seize thee, that they may slay thee. Arise then, and hasten for thy life; to the wilderness journey. The Lord thy God doth go with thee: He will not fail thee, He will not forsake thee. [Dt. 31:6] Now begone, and bless me also. [Ex. 12:32]

Elijah   Though stricken, they have not grieved! [Jer. 5:3] Tarry here my servant: the Lord be with thee. [1 Samuel 17:37] I journey hence to the wilderness. [1 Kgs. 19:4]

No 26 AIR

Elijah   It is enough, O Lord; now take away my life, for I am not better than my fathers! [1 Kgs. 19:4†] I desire to live no longer: now let me die, for my days are but vanity! [Job 7:16]

I have been very jealous for the Lord God of hosts; for the children of Israel have broken Thy covenant, thrown down Thine altars, and slain Thy prophets with the sword: and I, even I only, am left; and they seek my life to take it away. [1 Kgs. 19:10]

No 27 RECITATIVE

See, now he sleepeth beneath a juniper tree in the wilderness: [1 Kgs. 19:5] and there the angel of the Lord encampeth round about all them that fear Him. [Ps. 34:7]

No 28 TRIO

Angels Lift thine eyes to the mountains, whence cometh help. Thy help cometh from the Lord, the Maker of heaven and earth. He hath said, thy foot shall not be moved: thy keeper will never slumber. [Ps. 121:1,2,3†]

No 29 CHORUS

Angels He, watching over Israel, slumbers not nor sleeps. [Ps. 121:4] Shouldst thou, walking in grief, languish; He will quicken thee. [Ps. 138:7]

No 30 RECITATIVE

An Angel Arise, Elijah, for thou hast a long journey before thee. Forty days and forty nights shalt thou go; to Horeb, the mount of God. [1 Kgs. 19: 7,8†]

Elijah O Lord, I have laboured in vain; yea, I have spent my strength for naught, and in vain! [Isa. 49:4]

O that Thou wouldst rend the heavens, that Thou wouldst come down; that the mountains would flow down at Thy presence, to make Thy name known to Thine adversaries, through the wonders of Thy works! [Isa. 64:1,2]

O Lord, why hast Thou made them to err from Thy ways, and hardened their hearts that they do not fear Thee? [Isa. 63:17] O that I now might die! [1 Kgs. 19:4]

No 31 AIR

O rest in the Lord; wait patiently for Him; [Ps. 37:7] and He shall give thee thy heart's desires. [Ps. 37:4*] Commit thy way unto Him, and trust in Him, [Ps. 37:5†] and fret not thyself because of evildoers. [Ps. 37:1]

No 32 CHORUS

He that shall endure to the end, shall be saved. [Matthew 24:13]

No 33 RECITATIVE

Elijah Night falleth round me, O Lord! Be not Thou far from me! [Ps. 22:19†] hide not Thy face, O Lord, from me; my soul is thirsting for Thee, as a thirsty land. [Ps. 143:7,6]

An Angel Arise now! get thee without, stand on the mount before the Lord; [1 Kgs. 19:11] for there His glory will appear and shine on thee; Thy face must be veiled, [1 Kgs. 19:13†] for He draweth near.

No 34 CHORUS

Behold! God the Lord passed by! And a mighty wind rent the mountains around, brake in pieces the rocks, brake them before the Lord: but yet the Lord was not in the tempest. [1 Kgs. 19:11]

Behold! God the Lord passed by! And the sea was upheaved, and the earth was shaken: but yet the Lord was not in the earthquake. [1 Kgs. 19:11]

And after the earthquake there came a fire: but yet the Lord was not in the fire. [1 Kgs. 19:12]

And after the fire there came a still small voice; [1 Kgs. 19:12] and in that still voice, onward came the Lord.

No 35 RECITATIVE

Above Him stood the Seraphim, and one cried to another: [Isa. 6:2,3]

QUARTET AND CHORUS

Angels Holy, holy, holy is God the Lord – the Lord Sabaoth! Now His glory hath filled all the earth. [Isa. 6:3]

No 36 RECITATIVE AND CHORUS

Chorus Go, return upon thy way! [1 Kgs. 19:15] For the Lord hath yet left Him seven thousand in Israel, knees which have not bowed to Baal: [1 Kgs. 19:18] go, return upon thy way; thus the Lord commandeth.

RECITATIVE

Elijah I go on my way in the strength of the Lord. [Ps. 71:16] For Thou art my Lord; and I will suffer for Thy sake. [Ps. 16:2] My heart is therefore glad, my glory rejoiceth, and my flesh shall also rest in hope. [Ps. 16:9]

No 37 AIR

Elijah For the mountains shall depart, and the hills be removed; but thy kindness shall not depart from me, neither shall the covenant of Thy peace be removed. [Isa. 54:10]

No 38 CHORUS

Then did Elijah the prophet break forth like a fire; his words appeared like burning torches. [Ecclus. 48:1†] Mighty kings by him were overthrown. [Ecclus. 48:6†] He stood on the mount of Sinai, and heard the judgements of the future; and in Horeb, its vengeance. [Ecclus. 48:7†]

And when the Lord would take him away to heaven, [2 Kgs. 2:1] lo! there came a fiery chariot, with fiery horses; and he went by a whirlwind to heaven. [2 Kgs. 2:11]

No 39 AIR (Tenor)

Then shall the righteous shine forth

as the sun in their heavenly Father's realm. [Mt. 13:43] Joy on their head shall be for everlasting, and all sorrow and mourning shall flee away for ever. [Isa. 51:11]

No 40 RECITATIVE

Behold, God hath sent Elijah the prophet, before the coming of the great and dreadful day of the Lord. And He shall turn the heart of the fathers to the children, and the heart of the children unto their fathers; lest the Lord shall come and smite the earth with a curse. [Malachi 4:5,6]

No 41 CHORUS

But the Lord, from the north has raised one, who from the rising of the sun shall call upon His name and come on princes. [Isa. 41:25]

Behold my servant and mine elect, in whom my soul delighteth! [Isa. 42:1] On him the Spirit of God shall rest: the spirit of wisdom and understanding, the spirit of might and of counsel, the spirit of knowledge and of the fear of the Lord. [Isa. 11:2]

QUARTET

O! come every one that thirsteth, O come to the waters: come unto Him. O hear, and your souls shall live for ever! [Isa. 55:1,3]

No 42 CHORUS

And then shall your light break forth as the light of morning breaketh; and your health shall speedily spring forth then; and the glory of the Lord ever shall reward you. [Isa. 58:8†]

Lord, our Creator, how excellent Thy Name is in all the nations! Thou fillest heaven with Thy glory. [Ps. 8:1] Amen!

Note that Ecclus. refers to Ecclesiasticus (in the Apocrypha), not Ecclesiastes, as given by Bartholomew.

VORWORT

GESCHICHTE

Der erste Hinweis auf die Möglichkeit der Komposition eines Oratoriums, dem der Elias-Stoff zugrunde liegt, findet sich in einem Brief Mendelssohns an seinen Freund Karl Klingemann, der ihm half, eine Aufführung des *Paulus* in Liverpool vorzubereiten. Er datiert vom 12. August 1836 und enthält den Satz: 'Wenn Du Dir doch nur so viele Gedanken und Sorgen um einen "Elias" oder einen "Petrus" oder sogar einen "Og im Baschan" machen könntest, wie Du sie Dir jetzt um "Paulus" machst.'[1] Am 18. Februar 1837 schrieb Mendelssohn wieder an Klingemann: 'Am liebsten wäre es mir, wenn Du Dich des "Elias" annähmest – gliedere die Geschichte in zwei oder drei Teile, schreibe sie in Chöre und Arien aus, entweder in Versen oder in Deiner eigenen Prosa, oder stelle sie aus den Psalmen und den Propheten zusammen, mit mächtigen großen Chören, und schicke sie mir dann. ... Du kannst sie so dramatisch werden lassen wie "Judas Makkabäus", oder episch, oder beides zusammen.'[1] Im Herbst 1837 kam Mendelssohn anläßlich des Birmingham Festivals nach England und wohnte bei Klingemann. Die beiden verbrachten die meiste Zeit über einer Skizze eines Oratoriums, das auf 'Elias' basierte. Klingemann sollte sie dann vervollständigen. Bis zum Frühjahr 1838 war jedoch nicht mehr an der Skizze gearbeitet worden und sie wurde an Mendelssohn zurückgeschickt.

Im Herbst 1838 gewann Mendelssohn seinen Freund, Pfr. Julius Schubring, zur Mitarbeit. Am 31. Oktober sandte Schubring einen Entwurf des ersten Teils an Mendelssohn. Er fügte einige Kommentare bei, wie zum Beispiel: 'Ich habe überall versucht, wenn dies auch nicht immer möglich war, Stücke einzuführen, die nicht nur für die jeweilige Situation geeignet sind, sondern die möglicherweise auch in den Herzen der Hörer ein Echo wachrufen.'[2] Am nächsten Tag schrieb er ausführlicher: '... die Sache wird zu objektiv – ein interessantes, ja sogar mitreißendes Bild, das jedoch weit davon entfernt ist, das Herz des Zuhörers zu erbauen ... Deshalb solltest Du gründlich überlegen, ob Du es dieses Mal vorziehst, Dich von der Kirchenmusik (d.h. Musik, die erquickt, tröstet) abzuwenden, und ein Tongemälde wie die "Blocksberg-Kantate" [Walpurgisnacht] zu schaffen. Wenn nicht, so müssen wir uns eiligst daran machen, das dramatische Element zurückzuhalten und das geistliche zu verstärken, und uns immer um letzteres bemühen.'[2] Mendelssohns Antwort vom 2. November gibt wertvolle Hinweise auf seine Gedankengänge: 'Ich stelle mir Elias als einen vollkommenen Propheten vor, einen, den wir in unseren Tagen auch wieder gebrauchen könnten – energisch und begeisternd, aber auch ernst, zornig und traurig; ein bemerkenswerter Gegensatz zum Mob am Königshof und Pöbelhaufen im Volk – genaugenommen steht er im Gegensatz zur ganzen Welt und wird dennoch auf Engelsflügeln getragen. – – – Es freut mich zu hören, daß Du die herzergreifenden Gefühle der Schriftworte heraussuchst; aber wenn ich eine

Bemerkung machen dürfte, so sähe ich das dramatische Element gern mehr im Vordergrund sowie überschwenglicher und schärfer abgegrenzt – Bitte und Erwiderung, Frage und Antwort, plötzliche Unterbrechungen, etc. etc.'[3] Angesichts der Probleme, die Mendelssohn später mit der Witwen-Szene (No 8) hatte, ist die folgende Bemerkung aus demselben Brief von Interesse: 'Die Weglassung des Teils der Witwe und des Raben ist zweifellos ratsam; und auch die Kürzung des ganzen Anfangs, damit man auf den Hauptpunkten nach Herzenslust verweilen kann.'[3] Am 17. November sandte Schubring eine Skizze des zweiten Teils. Er war sichtlich beunruhigt über Mendelssohns Bemerkungen: 'Ich bin mehr und mehr davon überzeugt, daß Du den größten Teil des Textes selbst besorgen mußt. Wie soll ich wissen, was Dir je nach Anlaß durch den Kopf geht?' Mendelssohns Antwort (6. Dezember) unterstrich seinen Standpunkt noch stärker: 'Bezüglich des dramatischen Elements scheinen wir immer noch unterschiedlicher Meinung zu sein. Bei einer Person wie "Elias" scheint es mir, daß das dramatische Element vorherrschen sollte, wie auch bei allen anderen Personen des Alten Testaments, eventuell mit Ausnahme von Moses. Die Personen sollten so handeln und sprechen wie lebendige Personen – laß sie um Himmels willen nicht ein musikalisches Bild sondern eine wirkliche Welt sein, wie Du sie in jedem Kapitel des Alten Testaments findest. Das nachdenkliche und pathetische Element, das Du begehrst, sollte unserem Verständnis ausschließlich durch die Worte und Stimmungen der handelnden Personen nahegebracht werden.' Es findet sich kein weiterer Brief Schubrings über Elias in diesem Jahr. Erst im Februar 1839 deutet er in einem Brief an, daß das Thema, zumindest unter Mendelssohns Bedingungen, zuviel für ihn ist. Sechs Jahre lang tat sich dann nichts mehr.

Am 11. Juni 1845 faßte das Komitee des Birmingham Festivals den folgenden Entschluß: 'Es erscheint dem Komitee wünschenswert, Dr. Mendelssohn als Dirigenten für das nächste Festival zu gewinnen. Auch sollte er gefragt werden, ob er aus diesem Anlaß ein neues Oratorium oder ein anderes Stück komponieren kann.' (Mendelssohn war bei früheren Festivals anwesend gewesen, 1837 mit *Paulus* und 1840 mit dem *Lobgesang*). Am 24. Juli antwortete Mendelssohn und nahm die Einladung bis auf weiteres an. Er fügte hinzu: 'Ich habe vor einiger Zeit ein neues Oratorium angefangen und hoffe, es zu Ihrem Festival uraufführen zu können, aber es steckt erst in den Anfängen und ich kann Ihnen nicht versprechen, daß ich rechtzeitig damit fertig werde.'[4] Am 19. Oktober schrieb Mendelssohn wieder an das Birminghamer Komitee: 'Ich bin mir noch im Unklaren darüber, ob ich in der Lage sein werde, mein neues Oratorium rechtzeitig zu Ihrem Festival fertigzustellen. Ich hätte daran nicht gezweifelt, wenn ich weiter ungestört in Frankfurt hätte arbeiten können wie zu Beginn. Es gibt hier, in Dresden, und in Berlin jedoch so viele Angelegenheiten, die während der letzten Monate meine ganze Freizeit in Anspruch genommen haben, so daß ich damit nicht weitergekommen bin. Wenn diese Geschäfte weiter so anhalten (was ich jedoch nicht hoffe), so werde ich *nicht* in der Lage sein, mein Oratorium rechtzeitig zu beenden. Wenn sie jedoch *nicht* weiter anhalten, *werde* ich es rechtzeitig fertigstellen.'[4] Madame Sainton-Dolby (die in der ersten Aufführung der geänderten Fassung des *Elias* mitsang) erzählte eine Geschichte, die einen Eindruck gibt von dem Zustand der Komposition zu jener Zeit. Während eines Diners in Leipzig, wo sie am 25. Oktober 1845 auftreten sollte, saß sie neben Mendelssohn, der zu spät kam. 'Er entschuldigte sich und sagte, er habe fleißig an seinem Oratorium gearbeitet. Indem er sich an mich wendete, berichtete er, "Ich habe die Baßstimme skizziert, und nun auch die Altstimme." "Oh," rief ich aus, "sagen sie mir bitte, wie diese aussehen wird, denn ich interessiere mich besonders für diese Stimme." "Nur keine Angst," antwortete er, "sie wird ihnen gut liegen, denn sie ist eine typische Frauenstimme – halb Engel und halb Teufel." Ich wußte nicht, ob das als Kompliment gemeint war, aber wir lachten herzlich darüber.'[6]

Am 16. Dezember 1845 schickte Mendelssohn einen Entwurf des Librettos an Schubring und flehte ihn um Hilfe an. (Die Übersetzung von Lady Wallace datiert diesen auf 1842, aber Edwards hält dies für einen Fehler). Sein Brief scheint eine Wende in Richtung auf Schubrings Wunsch nach mehr Erbauung und weniger Drama anzudeuten. Er schließt: 'Der zweite Teil befindet sich, besonders gegen Ende, noch in einem sehr unfertigen Zustand. Ich habe bis jetzt noch keinen Schlußchor; was würdest Du dafür vorschlagen?'[3] Schubring machte einige Vorschläge und meinte 'die Ouvertüre, die eine Hungersnot darstellt, muß einen Zeitraum von drei Jahren umspannen.'[2] Mendelssohns Brief an Schubring vom 23. Mai 1846, nur drei Monate vor der Erstaufführung, zeigt, daß Mendelssohn immer noch mit dem zweiten Teil unzufrieden war, obwohl 'ich mit dem ersten Teil ziemlich fertig bin, und schon sechs oder acht Nummern des zweiten geschrieben habe. An einigen Stellen im zweiten Teil benötige ich jedoch eine Anzahl von wirklich schönen Schriftstellen, und ich flehe Dich an, sie mir zu schicken! Ich fahre heute abend an den Rhein, es hat also keine Eile; aber in drei Wochen bin ich wieder hier, und möchte dann sofort wieder an der Komposition arbeiten und sie fertigstellen.'[3] Der erste Teil war in Wirklichkeit am selben Tag nach England geschickt worden. Er fährt in seinem Brief fort: 'Jetzt beginnt der zweite Teil aber mit den Worten der Königin, "Die Götter sollen mir dies und das antun", etc. (1. Kön xix: 2); und die nächsten Worte, die mir keine Sorge bereiten, sind jene in der Wüstenszene (selbes Kapitel, 4ff), aber zwischen beiden benötige ich *erstens* etwas, das die Verfolgung des Propheten näher beschreibt; zum Beispiel hätte ich gern einige Chöre, die *gegen* ihn gerichtet sind und das Volk in seiner Launenhaftigkeit sowie den wachsenden Widerstand gegen Elias zeigen. *Zweitens*

fehlt mir eine Darstellung des dritten Verses des selben Abschnittes, zum Beispiel ein Duett mit dem Jungen, der Ruths Worte "Wo Du hingehst, will auch ich hingehen," etc. spricht. Aber was könnte Elias vorher und nachher sagen? Und was könnte der Chor vortragen? Kannst Du mir erstens ein Duett und einen Chor in diesem Sinn beschaffen? Bis Vers 15 ist dann alles in Ordnung, aber dort benötige ich einen Passus für Elias, zum Beispiel so etwas wie: "Herr, Dein Wille geschehe" (das steht, glaube ich, nicht in der Bibel), denn ich möchte, daß er *nach* der Erscheinung des Herrn seine völlige Ergebenheit verkündet, und nach all seiner Verzweiflung erklärt, zutiefst gefügig und Willens zu sein, seine Pflicht zu tun. Mir fehlen auch noch einige Worte, die er während seines Aufstiegs, vorher oder sogar nachher spricht, und auch einige Worte für den Chor. Der Chor beschreibt die Himmelfahrt mit den Worten aus 2. Kön ii: 11, aber ich benötige noch zwei sehr festliche Chöre. "Gott stieg empor unter Jubel" (Psalm xlvii:5) paßt nicht, da ja Elias und nicht der Herr empor gestiegen ist, aber etwas in *dieser* Art. Am Ende würde ich gerne noch einmal die Stimme von Elias hören ... Die Passagen, die Du mir für den Schluß des Ganzen geschickt hast (besonders das Trio zwischen Petrus, Johannes und Jakob) sind zu historisch und zu weit entfernt von der Gruppierung der (alttestamentarischen) Geschichte. Diese Schwierigkeit könnte ich jedoch dadurch umgehen, daß ich einen Chor anstelle eines Trios zu diesen Worten komponiere. Das läßt sich leicht bewerkstelligen und ich denke, daß ich das wahrscheinlich tun werde.'[3] Schubrings Antwort kam eine Woche später, und war sichtlich hilfreich. Er war jedoch immer noch der Meinung, 'das Oratorium darf nur einen neutestamentlichen Schluß haben. Elias muß dabei behilflich sein, den alten Bund in einen neuen zu verwandeln – daraus leitet sich seine große historische Bedeutung ab.'[2]

F.G. Edwards zitiert zahlreiche Briefe, die zeigen, wie hart Mendelssohn im Frühjahr 1845 am Arbeiten war: an Hauser aus Wien – 'Ich sitze bis über beide Ohren an meinem "Elias", und wenn er nur halb so gut wird, wie ich manchmal denke, werde ich sehr glücklich sein! Der erste Teil wird in den nächsten Tagen so ziemlich fertig und auch ein guter Teil des zweiten. Es gefällt mir nichts besser, als den ganzen Tag Noten zu schreiben. Oft komme ich so spät zum Essen, daß mich die Kinder mit Gewalt aus meinem Zimmer holen.'[6] An Jenny Lind – 'Während der letzten Wochen bin ich ein bißchen zerstreut geworden durch die Niederschrift der vielen Noten, die ich zuvor in meinem Kopf hatte, und die ich nun ab und zu aufs Papier zu einem Stück zusammenfüge, wenn auch nicht immer in der richtigen Reihenfolge, eine nach der anderen.'[6] An seine Schwester Fanny – 'Ich bin mehr unter Druck als sonst, da ein großer Teil des "Elias" noch nicht kopiert ist, während der erste Teil schon in England geprobt wird ... Morgen werde ich mich einschließen und mich nicht von der Stelle rühren bis der "Elias" fertig ist, was noch drei Wochen dauern mag, das schwöre ich auch beim Barte des Propheten.'[7]

Der folgende Brief, den Mendelssohn an Moscheles (Leiter des Festivals) schrieb, ist insofern bedeutsam, als er Licht auf den Charakter des Komponisten wirft. 26. Juni 1846: 'Mein lieber Freund – Der Anlaß für diese Zeilen ist eine Passage in Herrn Moores Brief. Er sagt: "Fast das gesamte Philharmonische Orchester ist [für Birmingham] verpflichtet worden, mit Ausnahme einiger weniger, die während Ihres Aufenthalts unangenehm aufgefallen sind." [1844 während einer Probe der Philharmoniker]. Ich protestiere schärfstens gegen diese Einschränkung. Da ich annehme, daß Du Deinen Einfluß in dieser Sache spielen lassen kannst, richte ich meinen Protest an Dich, und würde Dich bitten, ihn an Herrn Moore weiterzuleiten. Ich hasse nichts mehr, als vergangene Meinungsverschiedenheiten wiederaufleben zu lassen. Es ist schlimm genug, daß sie überhaupt stattfanden. Jene mit den Philharmonikern sind, was mich anbelangt, tot und begraben, und dürfen auf keinen Fall die Auswahl für das Birmingham Festival beeinflußen. Wenn Männer wegen ihrer Unfähigkeit zurückgewiesen werden, so geht mich das nichts an und ich kann dazu nichts sagen. Werden sie jedoch abgelehnt weil sie "während meines Aufenthalts unangenehm aufgefallen sind", so betrachte ich dies als eine Ungerechtigkeit, gegen die ich protestiere. Ich bin mir sicher, daß weitere Störungen seitens dieser Herren nicht zu befürchten sind. Das ist zumindest meine Überzeugung, die wahrscheinlich von allen Beteiligten geteilt wird. Ich wäre Dir sehr zu Dank verpflichtet, wenn Du dafür sorgen könntest, daß die Auswahl genauso vorgenommen wird, wie wenn ich nicht nach England käme. Die einzige Rücksicht, die man auf mich nehmen soll ist die, mich überhaupt nicht zu berücksichtigen. Du tätest mir einen großen Gefallen, wenn Du an Herrn Moore appellieren würdest, und ihn bitten könntest, die Sache ruhen zu lassen. Will man meine Wünsche befolgen, so muß der Vorfall hiermit vergessen werden. Sollte dies jedoch nicht der Fall sein, so werde ich mit einem Dutzend Briefe gegen diesen rachsüchtigen Geist protestieren. Entschuldige bitte all dies. – Immer, Dein Felix.'[3,8] (Joseph Moore war der Manager des Birmingham Festivals).

William Bartholomew (vgl. **Die Übersetzung**, unten) teilte Mendelssohn am 23. Juni in einem Brief mit, daß die Chöre des ersten Teils 'sich an diesem Tag in den Händen der Notenstecher befinden.' Sie müssen bemerkenswert schnell gearbeitet haben, denn, so Edwards, 'Herr Stimpson (der Chorleiter) erhielt die erste Lieferung der Chorstimmen erst gegen Mitte Juni, nur zwei Monate vor dem Festival. Obwohl diese gedruckt waren (der Rest des Oratoriums wurde von MS. Kopien gesungen und gespielt), war es wegen der vielen Änderungen – schwarze, rote und blaue Tinte war sehr großzügig benutzt worden, um die Änderungen und Abänderungen in den Stimmen zu markieren – nicht einfach, sie zu entziffern.' Viele dieser Änderungen fanden wahrscheinlich statt, nachdem Bartholomew Mendelssohns Brief vom 3. Juli erhalten hatte; seine erste Liste mit detaillierten Kommentaren zur Übersetzung des ersten Teils. 'Am 3. August, dreiundzwanzig Tage vor der Aufführung, trafen erst die ersten beiden Chöre des zweiten Teils ein, und der letzte Chor kam erst neun Tage vor dem Festival an!' (Edwards).

Die Uraufführung fand am Morgen des 26. August 1846 im Birminghamer Rathaus unter der Leitung des Komponisten statt. Sie war ein überwältigender Erfolg, obwohl die Sopranistin, Madame Caradori-Allen, Mendelssohn einiges Kopfzerbrechen bereitet hatte. Während der ersten Probe (mit Klavier, am 19. August in London) bat sie ihn 'Höre, Israel' einen Ton nach unten zu transponieren (Mendelssohn hatte Jenny Lind im Sinn als er dies komponierte) und weitere Änderungen vorzunehmen, da es 'kein Lied für eine Dame' sei! Mendelssohn klärte diese Situation, indem er damit drohte, eine andere Sängerin zu verpflichten. (Madame Caradoris Gage war genausohoch wie die Mendelssohns!). Am 20. und 21. August fanden Orchesterproben in den 'Hanover Square Rooms' statt. (Die Stimmen waren in Leipzig ausprobiert und korrigiert worden). Am 24. August fand im Birminghamer Rathaus eine vollständige Probe statt. Das *Birmingham Journal* berichtet 'Mendelssohn äußerte sich nach der Oratorienprobe sehr zufrieden mit der Art und Weise, mit der die Ausführenden sein Werk wiedergegeben hatten und gratulierte ihnen zu ihrer außerordentlichen Tüchtigkeit.' Aber 'auf Mendelssohns Wunsch fand am Dienstagabend anstelle des sonst üblichen Konzerts eine weitere Probe des "Elias" statt.' (Edwards). Es war eine Aufführung großen Stils: 125 Orchestermitglieder, 93 Streicher und verdoppelte Holzbläser; 79 Sopranistinnen, 60 Altisten (alles Männer), 60 Tenöre und 72 Bassisten. Hauptsolisten waren Madame Caradori-Allen, Fräulein Maria B. Hawes, Herr Charles Lockey, und Herr Staudigl. Obwohl James Stimpson, der Chorleiter, auch der offizielle Organist des Festivals war, war Dr. Henry Gauntlett speziell verpflichtet worden, die Orgel im *Elias* zu spielen.

Nach der Aufführung schrieb *The Times*: 'Die letzte Note des "Elias" ging im langanhaltenden, einstimmigen und ohrenbetäubenden Beifallssturm unter. Es war als ob seit langem gezügelte Begeisterung plötzlich die Ketten gesprengt hatte und nun den Saal mit Jubelrufen erfüllte. Mendelssohn, der davon sichtlich überwältigt war, bedankte sich und stieg schnell vom Dirigentenpodium herunter. Aber er war gezwungen, unter Hurrarufen und erneutem Jubel noch einmal zu erscheinen. Noch nie hat es einen so vollkommenen Triumph gegeben – noch nie eine gründlichere und schnellere Anerkennung eines großen Kunstwerks.' Mendelssohns Bemerkungen nach der Aufführung in einem Brief an eine Freundin (Frau Livia Frege aus Leipzig) geben wertvolle Aufschlüsse über seine Absichten im allgemeinen und in diesem Werk im besonderen: die Sopranstimme 'war so schön, so gefällig, so elegant und zugleich so fade, herzlos, so geistlos, so seelenlos, so daß die Musik einen liebenswürdigen Tonfall annahm, über den ich mich heute noch ärgere, wenn ich daran denke. Die Altstimme hatte nicht genug Volumen, um den Raum zu füllen ... aber ihr Vortrag war musikalisch und intelligent; damit kann ich mich eher abfinden als mit überhaupt keiner Stimme. So eine kalte, herzlose, musikalische Koketterie ist nicht nach meinem Geschmack. Sie ist etwas so Unmusikalisches und wird dennoch als Grundlage des Singens und Musizierens, ja der Musik überhaupt, angesehen.'[3,6]

Unmittelbar nach der Aufführung fing Mendelssohn mit der Arbeit an der Klavierbearbeitung an, und überarbeitete während der folgenden Monate einen Großteil des Werks. Er schreibt in einem Brief an Klingemann vom 6. Dezember 1846: 'Ich habe angefangen, mit meiner ganzen Kraft, an meinem "Elias" zu arbeiten, und hoffe den größten Teil dessen, was ich während der Aufführung als mangelhaft empfand, verbessern zu können ... Ich werde ernsthaft all jenes ändern, das mir nicht gefallen hat, und hoffe, das Ganze binnen weniger Wochen abschließen zu können, damit ich mit der Arbeit an etwas Neuem beginnen kann. Die Teile, die ich schon umgearbeitet habe, zeigen mir wieder, daß ich recht habe nicht zu ruhen bis das Werk so gut ist, wie es in meiner Kraft steht, obwohl nur sehr wenige Leute interessiert sind, von solchen Dingen zu hören, oder sie bemerken, auch wenn sie soviel Zeit in Anspruch nehmen. Aber der Eindruck, den solche Passagen hinterlassen und auf das ganze Werk haben, wenn sie wirklich besser sind, ist so verschieden, daß ich sie einfach nicht so stehen lassen kann, wie sie zur Zeit geschrieben sind.'[1] Mendelssohns Aufrichtigkeit in diesen Zeilen zeigt sich auch in der Tatsache, daß er in demselben Brief schreibt: 'Ich habe eine der schwierigsten Partien (die Witwe) fast abgeschlossen', während er am 8. Februar an Bartholomew schrieb: 'Ich werde eine *neue Arie* für die Witwe schicken', und Bartholomews Übersetzung erst am 3. März bei Mendelssohn ankommt! (Bezüglich Einzelheiten der Überarbeitung siehe unten unter **Die Übersetzung**).

Im Frühjahr 1847 kehrte Mendelssohn nach England zurück, um die ersten Aufführungen des überarbeiteten Oratoriums zu dirigieren. Innerhalb von 15 Tagen fanden sechs Aufführungen statt, angefangen mit einer in der Exeter Hall in London am 16. April. Am 20. April dirigierte er eine Aufführung der Hargreaves Choral Society in der Free Trade Hall in Manchester. Er kehrte nach London zurück, um am 23. eine Aufführung des *Elias* und am 26. ein Orchesterkonzert zu leiten. Ungeachtet der Tatsache, daß für den 28. und 30. weitere Aufführungen des *Elias* in London geplant waren, reiste Mendelssohn nach Birmingham, um dort ebenfalls eine *Elias*-Aufführung zu dirigieren; sie fand zugunsten von James Stimpson statt, und Mendelssohn verlangte dafür weder eine Gage noch Spesen. All jenes belastete die angeschlagene Gesundheit des Komponisten nicht unerheblich. Bei seiner Rückkehr erfuhr er, daß seine Schwester Fanny im Alter von nur 41 Jahren gestorben war. Diese Anspannung war zu groß, und obwohl ein Urlaub in Schottland hilfreich gewesen zu sein scheint, starb Mendelssohn am 4. November 1847.

Die erste Aufführung in Deutschland fand am 9. Oktober 1847 in Hamburg unter Leitung von August Krebs (1804-1880) statt. Mendelssohn sollte am 3. November in Berlin und am 14. November in Wien Aufführungen des *Elias* dirigieren. Jenny Lind sollte in letzterer erstmals die Partie singen, die der Komponist für sie geschrieben hatte. Mendelssohn sagte jedoch seinen Berlin Auftritt ab, noch ehe ein schwerer Schlaganfall ihn am 1. November teilweise lähmte. Die Aufführung fand dennoch statt, geleitet von Julius Schneider. Das Wiener Konzert unter Leitung des Chorleiters Schmidl wurde auf den 12. November vorverlegt und war ein Gedenkkonzert; alle Teilnehmer trugen Trauerkleidung und Mendelssohns leeres Podium war mit einem schwarzen Tuch behängt; eine Partitur und ein Lorbeerkranz verzierten das Pult.

Zeitgenössische Bilder geben Anlaß zu der Vermutung, daß weder die Singakademie in Berlin noch der Saal des Musikvereins in Wien groß genug waren, um jene Massen aufzunehmen, derer man sich in Birmingham und London bedient hatte. Es scheint in der Tat ein grundlegender Unterschied zu bestehen, zwischen dem Einfluß den der *Elias* in England und in den deutschsprachigen Ländern ausübte. Während das Werk in England ein bedeutender Katalysator für die zunehmende Anzahl und Größe der Chöre war, scheint es in der Heimat des Komponisten nicht viel Erfolg gehabt zu haben. Die erste Aufführung in Leipzig im Gewandhaus, unter der Leitung von Julius Rietz (1812-77), einem langjährigen Mitarbeiter Mendelssohns, markierte den Anfang der abnehmenden Beliebtheit Mendelssohns in Deutschland. Diese Abnahme wurde nicht zuletzt durch die antisemitischen Ansichten der Anhänger Wagners beschleunigt. Das Gewandhaus war halbleer und die Zuhörer verhielten sich teilnahmslos.

Im Gegensatz dazu fand ein Jahr nach Mendelssohns Tod eine 'große Aufführung des *Elias* Oratoriums zugunsten der "Mendelssohn Stiftung für kostenlose Stipendien am Leipziger Konservatorium"' (laut *The Times* vom 16. Dezember 1848) in der Exeter Hall statt. Sie wurde von Jenny Lind veranstaltet und war ausverkauft. Lind nahm nicht nur selbst daran teil, sondern ermunterte auch andere, ihre Dienst zur Verfügung zu stellen. Auch war sie maßgeblich an der Einrichtung des Mendelssohn-Stipendien-Fonds beteiligt, dessen erster Nutznießer Arthur Sullivan (1856) war.

Mendelssohns finanzielle Belohnung bestand aus 250 Guinees, die er von Edward Buxton von Ewer and Ewer für das englische Urheberrecht im *Elias* erhielt. Nach dem Tod des Komponisten schickte Buxton unaufgefordert weitere 100 Guinees an Mendelssohns Witwe. (350 Guinees entsprachen 1963 30,000 DM). Die Partitur, die Ewer im Juni 1847 veröffentlichte, kostete 36 Schillinge. Der Preis der ersten Oktavausgabe (1852) betrug 10 Schillinge; sie war sofort ein Verkaufsschlager.

DIE ÜBERSETZUNG

Das Libretto des *Elias* ist auf Deutsch geschrieben und basiert auf der Lutherbibel. Da das Werk in England aufgeführt werden sollte, wurde eine Übersetzung benötigt. Mendelssohn bat William Bartholomew (1793-1867), der schon viele andere Werke von Mendelssohn übersetzt hatte, dieselbe zu besorgen. Er beaufsichtigte einen großen Teil der Übersetzung sowohl des Originals als auch der bearbeiteten Fassungen durch englische Briefe. Alle Kommentare, die sich auf letztere beziehen, sind unten aufgelistet. Beide Männer hatten eindeutig großen Respekt vor den Fähigkeiten des anderen.

Anstelle von Zitaten aus den Briefen in chronologischer Reihenfolge, betrachte ich jede Nummer des Oratoriums der Reihe nach und gebe relevante Kommentare wieder. (M = von Mendelssohn an Bartholomew;[9] B = von Bartholomew an Mendelssohn.[10] Der Brief Mendelssohns vom 3.7.46* ist bei Edwards als Faksimile wiedergegeben; einige Kommentare von Bartholomew werden unten angeführt).

ERSTER TEIL

Einleitung Von Anfang an als Beginn des Oratoriums bestimmt. 'Ich möchte dieselbe, wenn möglich, so wie in der englischen Bibelfassung beibehalten und schlage deshalb vor:-'

(M 3.7.46).

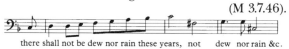

there shall not be dew nor rain these years, not dew nor rain &c.

Ouvertüre 'Ich hoffe, Sie werden Zeit haben, eine Ouvertüre oder eine Einleitung zu schreiben, es sei denn Sie wünschen ausdrücklich, daß es keine geben soll.' (B 23.6.46). 'Ich beabsichtigte, keine Ouvertüre zu schreiben, sondern gleich mit dem Fluch zu beginnen. Ich dachte das wäre sehr wirksam. Aber ich will mir Ihre Bemerkung bezüglich einer Einleitung auf jeden Fall durch den Kopf gehen lassen. Ich befürchte jedoch, daß dies eine sehr schwierige Aufgabe ist, und wüßte nicht, was man vor dem Fluch schreiben könnte oder sollte. Und nach ihm (ich spielte einmal mit dem Gedanken, die Ouvertüre *nach* dem Fluch einzufügen), *muß* der Chor sofort einsetzen.' (M 3.7.46) Bartholomew schrieb in einem späteren Brief: 'Ich habe lange darüber nachgedacht und Herr K[lingemann] und ich sind beide zu der Überzeugung gekommen, daß der Fluch als No 1 eine neue und interessante Spielart ist. Lassen Sie dann einen einleitenden Satz spielen, der ausdrucksvoll das Elend der Hungersnot beschreibt – denn der Chor setzt so unmittelbar nach dem Fluch ein, daß nicht genügend Zeit vorhanden zu sein scheint, um die gewünschten Ergebnisse zu produzieren.' Nachdem er aus diesem Brief zitiert hat schreibt F. G. Edwards: 'Es ist offensichtlich, daß Mendelssohn Bartholomew zu Dank verpflichtet ist für den Vorschlag, eine Ouvertüre zum "Elias" zu schreiben.' Man vergleiche dazu Schubring, der im Januar 1846 meinte: 'Die Ouvertüre, die eine Hungersnot darstellt, muß einen Zeitraum von drei Jahren umfassen.'

*Alle Daten erscheinen in der Form Tag. Monat. Jahr.

No 1 Viel wurde für 1847 geändert.

No 3 Die englische Version des ersten Satzes bereitete einige Probleme. Alle Originalausgaben geben die Zeile so wieder, wie im Hauptteil dieser Partitur, ohne Satzzeichen nach 'garments' [Kleider] und mit einem Doppelpunkt oder einem Semikolon nach 'transgressions' [Sünden]. Auch die jüngste Eulenberg Studienausgabe hat dieses beibehalten, obwohl Julius Rietz nach beiden Wörtern ein Komma gesetzt hat. Die alternative Fassung in dieser Partitur erscheint in der Novello Ausgabe für Singstimmen von 1885 und hat den Vorteil, daß sie plausibel klingt und dem Deutschen entspricht. Novello verwendete 1903 die geänderten Worte mit den unveränderten Satzzeichen, wodurch der Satz fast unverständlich wurde.

No 4 'Das Tempo is *Andante tranquillo*. Die ersten Worte stammen aus Jerem. xxix: 13, und die folgenden aus Hiob xxiii: 3, und ich möchte die letzten wörtlich beibehalten: "Oh, that I knew (*gebunden*) where I might find him, that (*zusätzliche* Note, wie Sie sie auch haben) I might come even to His Seat" (oder eventuell "presence", wenn die beiden Noten nicht gebunden werden sollen). [Wüßte ich doch, wie ich ihn finden könnte; gelangen könnte zu seiner Stätte.]' Bei Bartholomew stand: ' "Ah! could I find Him; and at His footstool bow before His presence." [Ach, daß ich ihn doch finden, und bei seinem Schemel vor seiner Gegenwart mich verbeugen könnte]. Und ehe das erste Thema und die ersten Worte wiederkehren, können die Noten wie folgt geändert werden:-'

(M 3.7.46).

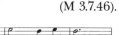

Oh, that I knew_ where I might find

Him. If with all, etc.

No 6 Für 1847 neu geschrieben.

No 7 'Lassen Sie den Anfang bitte so stehen wie in der Bibel, nämlich

For He shall give His *an-gels charge_* o-ver thee

und wenn Sie das Ende "and thus harm thee" [und dadurch dich verletzen] auslassen und es mit den Worten "against a stone" [an einen Stein] schließen könnten, so würde mir das besser gefallen.' (M 3.7.46). Das Ende war für 1847 geändert worden. 'Rezit. "Nun auch der Bach", Takt 9. Ich mag *Ihre* beiden Bindebögen am Ende nicht, und da Ihnen *meine* Notierung nicht gefällt, wie wäre es, wenn wir eine dritte Schreibweise ausprobierten? Nämlich:-

nei-ther shall the cruse of oil fail_

Nun bedienen Sie sich derer, die Ihnen von den *dreien* am besten gefällt.' (M 8.2.47).

No 8 Diese Szene wurde für 1847 völlig umge-schrieben. 'In den 13 Takten, die ich vor dem Chor "Wohl dem, der den Herrn fürchtet" [No 9] eingeschoben habe, und die aus Psalm cxvi und Deuteron. vi: 15 stammen, habe ich die deutschen Worte unter die englischen geschrieben, für den Fall, daß Sie die ursprüngliche Notation vorziehen. Auch habe ich hier und da ein Wort oder eine Silbe in der englischen Fassung eingeschoben, um ihr denselben Rhythmus wie in der deutschen Fassung zu geben. Dies hätte ich besonders gern in der gerade zitierten Passage, vor allem am Anfang von Elias' Antwort "Du sollst den", wo die zwei gebundenen Noten "Thou ♩ shalt" nicht gleich gut sind. Aber ich konnte nichts anderes finden und bin auch der Meinung, daß solche Stellen am besten so beibehalten werden, wie sie in der Bibel stehen.' (M 30.12.46). 'Ich gehe nicht auf die Takte 26 und 38 in No 8 ein, da Herr Buxton Sie wahrscheinlich davon unterrichtet hat, daß ich eine *neue Arie* für die Witwe schicken werde, und daß die gesamte No 8 daher bis dahin zurückgestellt werden muß. ... In Takt 157 [Seite 46, Takt 3], gefallen mir die beiden Hs und Cs über den Worten "render to the" nicht; könnte man dies nicht so schreiben:-

[Notenbeispiel: "What shall I ren-der to the"]

oder, wenn Ihnen das nicht gefällt, so sollte es wenigstens so geschrieben werden ·

[Notenbeispiel]

Ich muß jedoch gestehen, daß mir die *Achtel nicht gefallen, wenn man ohne sie auskommen könnte...*' (M 8.2.47). 'Mir gefallen alle Teile der Übersetzung, die Sie mir geschickt haben mit zwei Ausnahmen. ... in der neuen No 8 – die Worte aus Psalm vi, die Sie nur zögernd verwenden, kommen natürlich nicht in Frage. Ich lehne aber auch den zweiten Teil des Satzes ab, den Sie vorschlagen zu den Worten von Psalm xxxviii hinzuzufügen, nämlich: "I water my couch" etc. [ich netzte mit meinen Tränen meine Ruhestätte] – Mir gefällt das überhaupt nicht, zumal es in der deutschen Fassung so poetisch ist. Wenn Sie also einen Ersatz finden könnten, ohne "watering of the couch", der aber dennoch den Eindruck von Tränen, Nacht und Reinheit erweckt. Versuchen Sie es bitte!' (M. 3.3.47)

Die Witwe beschuldigt Elias, für die Krankheit ihres Sohnes verantwortlich zu sein, denn die Anwesenheit eines Mannes Gottes brächte verbor-gene Missetaten ans Licht. Gott könne sie nicht länger übersehen und fordere Vergeltung.

No 9 Geändert und für 1847 neu instrumentiert. 'Ist "the men" genauso biblisch wie "the man"? ['Gegen beides läßt sich etwas einwenden' B] Und falls kein Unterschied besteht, könnte der Satz eventuell lauten "Blessed is the man who fears Him, who delights", [Gelobt sei der, der Ihn fürchtet, der sich freut] und so weiter? Und was gefällt Ihnen besser: die Ausschmückung, "light shining over them", [Licht leuchtet über ihnen], oder stattdessen "to the upright", [den Rechtschaffenen] und die beiden Noten so zu binden:-

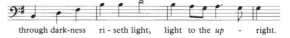

[Notenbeispiel: "through dark-ness ri-seth light, light to the up-right."]

['Das kling besser als "shining over them".' B] Bitte machen Sie es so, wie *Sie* es für richtig halten.' (3.7.46). 'Der folgende Chor, No 9, enthält ein bemer-kenswertes Beispiel für den *Bedeutungsunterschied* zwischen der deutschen und der englischen Fassung: die Worte "He is gracious", etc. [Er ist gnädig] (oder, wie Sie vorher schrieben, "they are gracious"), beziehen sich in Ihrer Version auf die Recht-schaffenen, während sie sich in unserer auf Gott beziehen. Der Abschnitt lautet daher bei uns, "Den Frommen geht das Licht auf *von* dem Gnädigen, Barmherzigen", etc. etc. Ich habe ihn auf jeden Fall mit letzterer Bedeutung komponiert, und die Frage ist nun, ob Sie es für weise halten, diesen einzuführen oder nicht. Ich schlug "Er ist" anstelle von "sie sind" vor, da ich annahm, daß man so die beiden Bedeutungen verstehen könnte; Ihnen wird aber höchstwahrscheinlich noch etwas viel besseres einfallen. Anstelle von "die sich an seinem Willen erfreuen" bevorzugte ich "die immer auf Friedens-wegen gehen" *nur* weil das ausdrucksvoller ist, und hoffe, daß Sie mir zustimmen. Dem Birminghamer Buch entnehme ich, daß Sie als Quelle für die Worte dieses Chorus' Psalm cvi: 3 angeben; ich habe sie jedoch den Psalmen cxxviii: 1, und cxii: 1 und 4 entnommen, obwohl fast derselbe Abschnitt auch in Psalm cvi: 3 vorkommt.' (M 30.12.46). 'Takt 10: Das zweifache F im Sopran gefällt mir nicht, obwohl ich Ihrer Beobachtung zustimme.' Ich schlage jedoch stattdessen vor:-

[Notenbeispiel: "Bless-ed {are the men / are they}"]

Sollte Ihnen das mißfallen, schlagen Sie bitte eine andere Schreibart vor, aber der Sopran *kann keine* zwei Fs haben während der Tenor auch zwei Fs hat. Takt 14 so wie *Sie* es vorschlagen. Anstelle von Takt 13 bei Ihnen und mir schlage ich vor:-'

(M 8.2.47).

[Notenbeispiel: "men who fear Him."]

No 10 Einige Änderungen für 1847. 'Zu Anfang hätte ich gern dieselben Worte wie in No 1, nämlich: "vor dem ich stehe", anstelle von "Wahrlich, ich sage Euch". Ich ziehe "der sei Gott" der Variation "der soll Gott sein" vor, die Sie in Bleistift ergänzt haben. Anstelle von "Ich aber bin allein übriggeblieben", schlage ich die folgende Änderung vor:

[Notenbeispiel: "I, e-ven I, on-ly re-main,"]

Wie Ihnen, gefällt mir auch "Ruft Eure Waldgötter", usw. besser.' (M 3.7.46).

Jezebel, die Frau von Ahab, war die Tochter des Königs von Tyre in Phönizien. Die Phönizier verehrten den Naturgott Melkart, den die Israeliten unter dem Namen Baal, wie auch alle anderen fremden Naturgötter, kannten. Als Jezebel Ahab heiratete, brachte sie ihre Religion mit ihren Götzen, Priestern und Propheten mit sich.

No 11 'Ist die Betonung auf "extirpate" nicht falsch? ['No' B]. Die Silbe "tir" ist immer die erste im Takt und die stärkste Silbe, mit betontem Akzent.' ['Und das soll sie auch sein' B] (M 3.7.46).

No 12

Or he is per-su-ing.

und dann –

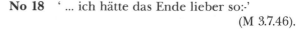

jour-ney; or per-ad - venture

(M 3.7.46).

No 13 'Könnten die Worte "ritz Euch mit Lanzen nach Eurer Weise" nicht beibehalten werden?' (M 3.7.46).

No 14 Einige Veränderungen für 1847.

No 15 'Ein Stück, bei dem ich wieder Ihre freundliche Hilfe benötige. Seitdem ich es erstmals für die Aufführung in Birmingham weggeschickt habe, bin ich der Meinung, daß es nicht so bleiben darf, wie es ist, mit den *Versen und Reimen*; das einzige Beispiel für einen lutherischen Choral in diesem alttestamentarischen Werk. Ich wollte eine Choralstimmung und meinte, daß ich ohne sie nicht auskomme, und dennoch wollte ich keinen Choral schreiben. Ich bediente mich letztendlich jener Psalmabschnitte, die am besten zu der Situation passen und komponierte in etwa demselben Stil und derselben Farbe. Ich war sehr glücklich als ich merkte (als ich in die englische Bibel schaute), daß der Anfang Wort für Wort so lautete wie in der deutschen. Kurz nach dem Anfang war meine Freude jedoch schnell verflogen und ich möchte Sie hier deshalb um Ihre Hilfe bitten. Die Worte stammen aus Psalm lv: 23; Psalm cviii: 5; und Psalm xxv: 3.' (M 30.12.46). 1846 lauteten sie: 'Erhör das Gebet Deines Dieners,/ während Engel vor Dir niederknien/ und die Welt um Deinen Thron herum Dich mit Lob überschüttet. / Oh hilf ihm in der Not, / leih' Ihm Dein gnädges Ohr – Jehovah, Sabaoth, / Du Schöpfer, Gott und Herr!' 'Die Musik war auch abgeändert worden; ihre quartettartige Choralform und karge Begleitung waren jedoch beibehalten worden.' (Edwards).

No 16 Sehr verändert für 1847. 'Könnte das Ende nicht so lauten: "wir sollen neben ihm Keine anderen Götter haben", oder "dem Herrn" (aus Exodus xx: 3)? ['Und wir *werden* keinen anderen Gott haben als Gott den Herrn' B]. Anstelle von "laßt keinen Propheten" schlage ich vor:' (M 3.7.46).

and let not one of them es-cape ye; *bring* them; &c

'Ich ergänzte die deutschen Worte ... in Bleistift, da

ich der Meinung war, daß die englische Übersetzung "adoring" [anbetend], usw. nicht ganz die richtige Bedeutung wiedergibt und auch nicht denselben Rhythmus wie das Deutsche hat, was durch den Takt, den ich vor der Pause eingeschoben habe, noch deutlicher wird. Unser "fallt nieder" bedeutet etwas schlimmeres, so meine ich, als "bow down" oder "to adore"; ich stelle jedoch infrage, ob es in Englisch wiedergegeben werden könnte oder sollte!' (M 30.12.46). 1846 lauteten die Worte: 'Bow down, bow down! on your faces fall adoring!'

No 18 ' ... ich hätte das Ende lieber so:-'
(M 3.7.46).

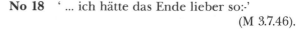

Woe un-to them, woe___ un-to them.

No 19

O Lord, Thou hast o - ver

thrown thine en - e-mies, and des-troy'd them! Now

look on us, &c.

Dann würde ich gerne die folgenden Noten ändern:-

Go up now, child, and look to-ward the

sea. Has my prayer_ been heard by the Lord?

Mir gefällt auch besser "the heavens are *as* brass" [der Himmel ist ehern] – man könnte eine Note hinzufügen. Anschließend schlage ich vor:-

clo - sed up, be - cause they have sinn'd___

_ have sin-ned a-gainst Thee

Und danach, wenn Sie "and turn from *their* sin" [und sich von *ihren* Sünden bekehren] vorziehen, so könnte man eine Note hinzufügen, um die Worte so wie in der Bibel zu belassen. Ich finde den folgenden Satz biblischer, wenn man die Worte wie in 2. Chron vi: 27 beläßt:-

Then hear from heav'n and for - give___ the sin,

Dann hätte ich die Noten gern folgendermaßen geändert:-

Go up a-gain, and still look to-wards the sea.

Und dann "the earth is *as* iron" [die Erde ist *wie*

Eisen]. Und wie würde Ihnen dann:-

There is a sound of a-bun-dance of rain.

gefallen. ['Geändert, aber nicht so, denn wenn er das Geräusch von Regen im Überfluß vernimmt, so braucht er nachher nicht mehr für die Antwort auf sein Flehen zu beten.' B. So wird die Szene allerdings in 1. Könige 18 geschildert. Interessant ist auch die folgende Bemerkung Mendelssohns in einem Brief an Paul, seinen Bruder, die sich auf die erste Aufführung bezieht: 'Wie oft ich während dieser Zeit an Dich gedacht habe! Besonders, jedoch wenn "das Geräusch von Regen im Überfluß" erklang ...'³]. Wenn möglich, so würde ich gerne "I implore Thee" [ich flehe Dich an] auslassen, das mir nicht sehr biblisch klingt. Sollte ich unrecht haben, so lassen Sie es bitte stehen; aber wenn nicht, so könnte man stattdessen die Worte "to my prayer" wiederholen. Das folgende stammt aus Psalm xxviii: 1:-

Un-to Thee will I cry, Lord, my

rock: be not si-lent to me.

und könnte der folgende Satz nicht lauten:-

{and Thy great mer - cies do re-mem-ber, O Lord!
{Thy gra-cious

['Änderung ja, aber nicht ganz so' B] Dann gefällt mir besser:-

like a man's hand!

Anstelle von "His boundless" schlage ich vor (die erste Note) G auszulassen und stattdessen "for His" zu schreiben und danach eine Note (A) zu ergänzen, damit es heißen kann "endureth *for* evermore" [währet ewiglich].' (M 3.7.46).

No 20 'Mir gefällt "der Herr ist *über* ihnen" besser als "ist der Höchste" .' (M 3.7.46).

ZWEITER TEIL

No 21 Ergänzt und neugeordnet für 1847. Der zweite Teil begann ursprünglich mit einem Tenorrezitativ, das für 1847 herausgenommen worden war. 'Das Rezitativ, das ich Ihnen hier schicke, stammt aus Jesaja xlix: 7. Zunächst bereiteten die englischen Worte keine Probleme, später paßten sie aber nicht und (was am wichtigsten war) hatten eine andere Bedeutung. Auf Deutsch heißt es, der Herr spricht "zu der tief verachteten Seele und *zu dem Volk*, das von anderen verachtet wird, und zu seinem Diener, der *von Tyrannen unterdrückt wird*". All jenes veranlaßte mich, diese Worte für das Rezitativ zu verwenden, und es ist mir deshalb sehr daran gelegen, daß die englische Fassung ebenfalls diese Bedeutung hat.' (M 30.12.46). 'Mir gefällt:-

Who_ hath be-liev-ed our re-port

dann:

-veal-ed to

besser. Es *muß* so aussehen:-

be not a-fraid, be

und nicht:

be not a -

was aber nicht zu dem schnellen Tempo des Satzes paßt. Takt 89 ist unmöglich wie Sie ihn vorschlagen, denn über a♯ und g♯ etc. dürfen keine Worte gesprochen werden; die Noten müßen gebunden sein, wie in der deutschen Fassung. Vor allem müssen sie auf einer guten Silbe gesungen werden (nicht "u", oder "o" etc.). Ich schlage deshalb vor:-

I, the Lord will strengthen Thee!

Auf jeden Fall flehe ich Sie an, *binden Sie die Noten*, denn das ist für das ganze Lied wichtig. Dasselbe gilt auch für die Wiederholung dieses Teils, Takt 140. Takt 148 muß so aussehen:-

for I thy

All jene Teile, die ich hier *nicht erwähnt* habe, sind, so wie Sie sie vorgeschlagen haben, ausgezeichnet.' (M 25.2.47).

Mendelssohn war deutlich besorgt um das kurze Rezitativ auf Seite 111; der Sinn, den er oben wiedergibt, wird in der New English Bible (1961-70) deutlich: 'Thus says the Holy one, the Lord who ransoms Israel' [so spricht der Herr, der Befreier Israels]. Das Ganze mag verständlicher werden, wenn man 'and' ausläßt, und 'his' die Viertelnote erhält, wie im Deutschen. Die ersten Ausgaben enthalten kein Komma nach 'Israel', um zu zeigen, wie es gelesen werden soll, und auch der Rhythmus macht dies dem Hörer nicht klar. Das Komma kommt bei Rietz und in allen späteren Ausgaben vor und verwirrt die Bedeutung noch mehr.

No 22 'So wird es doch dich nicht treffen'. Siehe Psalm 91: 5,6 bezüglich 'es'.

No 23 Überarbeitet für 1847.
'Die Sünden Jereboams'. Etwa sechzig Jahre bevor Ahab den Thron bestieg, wurde Jereboam der erste nördliche König eines geteilten Israels, als die zehn nördlichen Stämme sich gegen Solomons Sohn Reheboam auflehnten. Judah behielt zwei Stämme und Jerusalem. Jereboam mußte sich andere Opferstätten und goldene Kälber errichten als Zeichen der Gegenwart Jehovahs. Da der Stier (ein Naturgott und somit ein Baal), von den Kaanitern angebetet wurde, war dies der Anfang des Eindringens fremder Götter, die ihre erste Niederlage am Berg Karmel erlebte. Jezebels Vernichtung der Propheten Jehovahs war ein letzter Versuch, die Situation zu retten; er endete mit einer Niederlage.

No 24   Neu für 1847; der Chor, der 1847 an seiner Stelle stand, war außer Gebrauch gekommen.

No 25   Neu für 1847. Die vier Instrumentaltakte am Ende waren ein Nachgedanke – Bartholomew schrieb – 'Was halten Sie von einem (kurzen) Zwischenspiel, das Zeit für die Reise läßt? und dann, müde, könnte er vor lauter Müdigkeit sagen, "Es ist genug"!!'

No 27   Die englischen Psalmworte, wie sie bei Simrock stehen, sind ein wörtliches Zitat aus der Authorised Version (1611) und man hielt es nicht für nötig, sie in der Revised Version (1881-5) zu ändern. Im Book of Common Prayer (1662) steht 'The *angel* of the Lord tarrieth *round about* them that fear him' [der Engel des Herrn verweilt bei denen, die ihn fürchten]. Sogar die New English Bible enthält 'The *angel* of the Lord is on guard *round* those who fear him.' Alle späteren Fassungen folgten der Ewer Fassung mit ihren vielen Engeln, und das Simrock Exemplar in der British Library wurde ihr mit Bleistift ebenfalls angepaßt.

No 28   Ursprünglich ein Duett mit ganz anderer Musik.

No 30   [Takt 30] ' "that thou would'st please destroy me" [ach, daß Du mich zerstörtest] klingt sehr merkwürdig – ist es biblisch? Wenn es aus der Bibel stammt, so habe ich keine Einwände, aber wenn nicht, so würde ich Sie bitten, es durch etwas anderes zu ersetzen.' (M 3.3.47)

No 31   'Könnten Sie in dem Lied, "O rest in the Lord" [Sei stille dem Herrn], die Worte "and He will ever keep the righteous" durch etwas ähnliches wie die Worte in Psalm 37, v.4 ersetzen!; "and He shall give thee" [der wird dir geben] paßt gut zu den Noten. Man muß dann nur noch den Ausdruck "the desires of thy heart" [deines Herzens Wünsche] etwas abändern, damit die Worte zur Musik und allem anderen paßen. Anstelle des Endes "He will defend thee", [er wird dich beschützen] etc., gefällt mir Psalm 37, v.8 auch besser, zum Beispiel so: "and cease from anger, and fret not thyself"; oder, "and cease from anger and forsake the wrath", [steh ab vom Zorn und laß den Grimm]. Ein oder zwei Noten müßten dann nur geringfügig geändert werden, ungebunden anstelle von gebunden und *umgekehrt*. Und ich bitte Sie, stellen Sie die *Betonung* immer voran, besonders in den *Chören*! Und den Liedern! Und den Rezitativen!' (M 21.7.46). Bartholomew hatte am 20. Juli 1846 an Mendelssohn geschrieben; sein Brief kreuzte sich mit dem eben zitierten: 'Kennen Sie eine schottische Air namens "Robin Gray"?

Young Ja - mie lov'd me well, and
ask'd me for his bride, &c.

Vergleichen Sie nun die Arie … damit.' Die ursprüngliche Fassung lautete so:

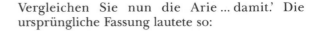

Sei stil - le dem Herrn, und war - te auf ihn.

Er vermerkt weiter, daß ihm und zwei Freunden diese Ähnlichkeit aufgefallen wäre, und führt Beispiele an

pound were both for me.   fuh - ren.

Mendelssohn antwortete ihm am 28. Juli 1846: 'Ich entsinne mich nicht, die schottische Ballade, die Sie erwähnen, je gehört zu haben, … da ich aber schon immer eine Abneigung (anderer Art) gegen mein Lied gehegt habe, und die Ballade sehr bekannt zu sein scheint, die Ähnlichkeit darüber hinaus sehr auffallend ist, so werde ich das Lied (wahrscheinlich) ganz auslassen … eventuell füge ich an seiner Statt ein anderes Lied ein, ich bezweifle das aber, und denke fast, daß diese Auslassung eine Verbesserung ist.' Bartholomew antwortete 'Warum wollen Sie das Lied "Sei stille" ganz auslassen, wenn doch die Änderung von ein oder zwei Melodienoten seine ganze Identität unkenntlich machen würde, und das Lied als Ganzes, so meine ich, nicht verdürbe? Wenn Sie es, insbesondere wegen meines Hinweises, weglassen, so würde mich das sehr schmerzen.' Dies geschah nach weiterer Diskussion.

Beachten sie Mendelssohns Tempo – Viertel, nicht Achtel, = 72.

No 33   'In dem Rezit. "Hear me speedily, O Lord", habe ich zu Anfang die Worte wie folgt geändert:-

Herr, es wird Nacht um mich! Sei du nicht

fer - ne!   Ver-birg dein etc.

1. Kön, xix: 9; Ps. xxii: 12, 20. Ändern Sie die englischen Worte bitte dementsprechend, und nehmen Sie bitte auch die folgenden Änderungen in der Musik dieses Rezitativs vor: Takt 16 (Begleitung) soll so aussehen:-

Takt 22 (Begleitung) so:-

Lento ten.

In Takt 24 soll die Stimme so ausschauen:-

face must be veil - ed.

und in Takt 27 (der letzte) folgendermaßen:·'

(M 2.2.47)

for He draw-eth near.

No 34 'Wieder möchte ich die Noten ändern, um den englischen Bibeltext beibehalten zu können. ... Den Anfang hätte ich gerne so geändert:·

And be-hold, the Lord passed by.

oder, wenn "passed" zwei Silben benötigt:·

Lord pass-ed

Das Ende der ersten Phrase "as he approached" [Takte 26-30] gefällt mir nicht so ganz; könnten Sie stattdessen nicht *vier* Silben finden (indem sie aus den zwei *gebundenen* Noten einzelne machen) – z.B., "as the Lord drew near" (lachen Sie nicht), oder etwas mit einem *starken, entschiedenen Akzent auf der letzten Silbe!* Dann folgt:·

But the Lord was not in the tem - pest.

Dann wieder: "Der Herr ging vorüber." Und am Ende wieder, "aber der Herr war nicht im Erdbeben." Auch beim dritten Mal: "aber der Herr war nicht im Feuer."

But the Lord, &c.

Dann:·

And af-ter the fire there came a still small voice—

(ich meine, es ist hier *ziemlich* wichtig, die biblischen Ausdrücke *zumindest* am Anfang beizubehalten!). Und dann vielleicht: "Und in dem Säuseln nahte sich der Herr."' (M 18.7.46). 'Ich ziehe:·

Be - hold, God the

und danach:·

But yet the

und ebenso:·

But yet the

vor, denn das Wort "God" sollte nicht über einer so kurzen Note und in solch einem Rhythmus stehen, wohingegen das unbedeutende Wort "yet" genau zu einer solchen kurzen Note paßt.' (M 26.9.46).

No 36 Neu für 1847.

'my glory': 'Der edelste Teil meines Wesens, Seele, Herz, rationales Leben; fähig, Gott zu loben; parallel zu Seele.' (A.H.McNeile, in 'A New Commentary on Holy Scripture', Hgg., Gore, Goudge und Guillaume, SPCK 1928). Diese Bedeutung steht nicht im Oxford English Dictionary aber ist eindeutig richtig.

No 37 'Die englischen Worte passen wörtlich zu meiner Musik.' (M 10.8.46).

No 38 'Mir gefällt: "sein Wort brannte *wie eine Fackel*" besser – ich lege so viel Wert auf die *Fackel*, da sie mehr als jedes andere Wort den F Moll Charakter des Anfangs erklärt.' (M 26.9.46). Bei F.G. Edwards findet sich die folgende Bemerkung: 'Es ist sehr schwer, die Gedankengänge eines Komponisten nachzuvollziehen; was *kann* bloß die Verbindung zwischen "Fackeln" und der F Moll Tonart sein?'

Horeb und Sinai sind verschiedene Namen für ein und denselben Berg, auf dem Elias in Nos. 30-36 des Oratoriums den Herrn traf. Der ganze Chor entstammt einem Abriß von Elias' Leben, der im ersten Teil von Kapitel 48 in Ecclesiasticus steht. Indem das erste Wort 'Then' (das im biblischen Zusammenhang bedeutet: nach den Taten Jereboams) durch 'Thus' ersetzt wird, mag dies deutlicher werden. Das deutsche Libretto ist ein wörtliches Zitat aus der lutherischen Bibel, und enthält 'Und' nicht 'Dann'. Die Übersetzung in der New English Bible ist verständlicher: 'You heard a denunciation at Sinai, a sentence of doom at Horeb.' [er hat auf dem Berge Sinai gehört die zukünftige Strafe und in Horeb die Rache].

No 40 Es ist erwähnenswert, daß die Zeitstufe dieses Zitats für das Oratorium geändert worden war. Maleachi prophezeite die zukünftige Rückkehr Elias' und beschrieb nicht seine vergangenen Taten. Er schrieb: 'Seht, ich *werde* Euch Elias schicken'. Da das Deutsche auch das Futur beibehält, mag es berechtigt sein, 'hath sent' [hat geschickt] in 'shall send' [wird schicken] umzuändern. 'He' im zweiten Satz bezieht sich auf Elias, nicht auf den Herrn.

No 41 'Der *zweite* Teil von No 41, "er wird öffnen die Augen der Blinden" muß ebenfalls ausgelassen werden. Die Worte "und der Furcht des Herrn" [Takte 52-3] gehen deshalb direkt in das Quartett in B Dur "Wohlan, denn" über.' [Dies war ein *alla breve* Satz mit 86 Takten]. (M 9.8.46). 'Ich ziehe die *zweite* Fassung des Anfangs von No 41 entschieden vor: "Aber der Herr hat *einen* von Norden erweckt!" (das ist sehr gut). Im letzten Takt, vor dem *Andante*, gefällt mir jedoch nicht

anstatt

Diese zwei langen Noten sind in der Tat *wichtig* für die Entwicklung der ganzen Phrase, so wie ich sie beabsichtigte. Könnte man jetzt nicht sagen "call His name", [seinen Namen rufen] anstelle von "call upon His name?" Dann wäre die Hauptschwierigkeit beseitigt. Und wäre es vielleicht möglich, "of the sun" auszulassen und nur zu sagen "from the rising" (das wird zumindest in unserer deutschen Bibel oft getan)? Der zweite Teil lautet dann auch fast so wie im Deutschen:-

And from the ri-sing he shall call His Name

Der Rest des *Andante con moto* paßt nun sehr gut mit der von Ihnen vorgeschlagenen Änderung zu meiner Musik. Ich hätte dort jedoch lieber die erste Fassung, und am Anfang (*Andante sostenuto*) die zweite Version. Und warum auch nicht? Das *Andante con moto* könnte dann so beginnen: "But the Lord hath upraised one, the Lord," etc. Wenn Ihnen das jedoch gegen den Strich geht, so belassen Sie hier auch die zweite Fassung. Denn der Anfang ist viel wichtiger. Mir gefällt:-

He shall call up - on His Name

besser.' [S. 191, Brief A]. (M 26.9.46). [Für Anmerkungen zum Zeitmaß siehe unten unter **Metronombezeichnungen**]. 'Über den Chor "But, saith the Lord, I have raised one", schreibe ich die deutsche Bezeichnung Schluss-Gesang – die sich sowohl auf diesen Chor als auch auf das folgende Quartett und den letzten Chor bezieht. Könnten Sie ein entsprechendes *englisches* Wort finden, das sich verwenden ließe? Es darf nicht Finale sein, denn das erinnert mich an eine Oper; es darf auch nicht "Final Chorus" [Schlußchor] sein, da es zwei Chöre und ein Quartett bezeichnen soll. Ich hätte aber gern ein Wort über diesen drei Stücken, um ihre Zusammengehörigkeit deutlich zu machen; eine Art "Epilog" im Gegensatz zum "Prolog" oder zur "Einleitung" vor der Ouvertüre.' (M 2.2.47).

Der ungewöhnliche Ausdruck 'come on princes' bedeutet wenig ohne den Rest des Verses; in der Revised Standard Bible steht 'he shall trample on rulers'. 'Trample' würde besser zur Musik passen als 'come on', und wäre auch viel verständlicher.

Auf Seite 190, Takte 6 und 7, finden sich bei Ewer die folgenden alternativen Harmonien in der Alt-, Tenor- und Klavierstimme:

Hier handelt es sich vermutlich um eine frühere Fassung, die im Manuskript, auf dem die Ewer Ausgabe beruht, nicht verbessert worden ist.

No 42 Völlig neu geschrieben zu neuen Worten.

Der anonyme Redakteur der Novello Ausgabe von 1903 brüstet sich damit, die englischen Worte 'ever shall reward you' in 'shall be thy rereward' umgeändert zu haben, da dieses viel Biblischer sei. In der Authorised Version steht: 'and thy righteousness shall go before thee: the glory of the Lord shall be thy rereward.' In der New English Bible wird der Ausgleich zwischen den beiden Phrasen deutlich: 'your own righteousness shall be your vanguard and the glory of the Lord your rearguard.' [Eure Rechtschaffenheit sei Eure Vorhut und die Herrlichkeit des Herrn Eure Nachhut]. Hätte der Redakteur die Schreibung der Revised Version verwendet – 'rearward' – so wäre dies deutlicher geworden, aber auch der zweite Satz allein klingt im Englischen wenig plausibel. Das Deutsche hat eine etwas andere Bedeutung – 'der Herr will sich Eurer annehmen' oder 'Euch führen' – was für sich stehen kann. Es ist auch möglich, daß Bartholomew (wie viele andere nach ihm) das Wort als 're-reward' und nicht 'rereward' interpretierte, und meinte, die Bedeutung damit eher zu verdeutlichen als sie zu verändern. Das Ergebnis ist dem Deutschen eindeutig näher und läßt sich leichter zu Musik setzen. Neuere Ausgaben der Fassung von 1903 tragen noch mehr zur Verwirrung bei, da sie in der Einleitung 'rereward' durch 'reward' ersetzen, 'rereward' jedoch im eigentlichen Chor stehen lassen!

METRONOMBEZEICHNUNGEN

F.G. Edwards gibt ein Faksimile einer Liste von Metronombezeichnungen wieder, die Bartholomew am 9.4.47 von Mendelssohn erhielt, anläßlich der ersten Aufführung des überarbeiteten *Elias* in der Exeter Hall. Es finden sich einige Unstimmigkeiten mit der dann gedruckten Fassung:

No 10 Zwischen dem *Allegro vivace* [Takt 14, erneut bei A und oben auf Seite 56] und dem *Maestoso* [7 Takte vor Buchstabe C] steht ein *Andante* ♩ = 72, vermutlich bei Buchstabe B.

No 30 *Allegro vivace* und *Allegro moderato* werden nur als *Allegro* und *Moderato* angegeben.

No 32 ♩ = 60, nicht 66.

No 33 *Andante* ♩ = 76, nicht 72.

No 40/41 Bei Simrock zählen Rezit. und Chor als No 40, das Quartett ist No 41; bei Ewer ist das Rezit. No 40, der Chor No 41 und das Quartett No 41a. Aus Mendelssohns Brief vom 26.9.46, der oben zitiert ist, wird deutlich, daß der Wechsel von *Andante sostenuto* zu *Andante con moto* sich im Takt 8 des Chors vollziehen soll und nicht am Anfang, wie es in beiden Partituren steht.

VORGEHENSWEISE DES HERAUSGEBERS

Es gibt kein vollständiges Autograph der Urfassung. Die Version des Kopisten, derer man sich in Birmingham bediente und die sich früher im Novello Archiv befand, wurde 1989 von der Granada Group während einer Phillips Auktion verkauft. Ein Autograph der Gesangsausgabe, die für die zweite Fassung ausgiebig überarbeitet worden war, wird in der Margaret Denecke Mendelssohn Sammlung in der Bodleian Library, Oxford (GB-Ob-MDM C.39) aufbewahrt. Das vollständige Autograph der überarbeiteten Fassung befindet sich in Krakau (PL-Kj-Bd, 51). Die vollständige Partitur war 1847 von Simrock mit deutschen und englischen Worten, die Vokalausgabe nur auf Deutsch, gedruckt worden. Ewer (später von Novello übernommen) druckte zur gleichen Zeit die Gesangsausgabe in Form eines wunderschön gebundenen und gedruckten Folios mit englischen Worten. Diese Ausgabe enthielt eine kurze Liste von Errata, die später korrigiert wurde als die Folioausgabe 1850 neu aufgelegt wurde. Von Ewer gibt es auch eine Gesangsausgabe im Oktavformat mit modernerem Druck sowie deutschen und englischen Worten, die der Katalog der British Library ebenfalls auf 1847 datiert, sowie eine überarbeitete Fassung von 1852. Die Ausgabe enthält kein Datum und scheint stellenweise verbessert worden zu sein, besonders die Satzzeichen. Es gibt einen großen Unterschied – die Ouvertüre wird in einer Fassung für zwei Klaviere wiedergegeben. Wahrscheinlich handelt es sich hier um eine spätere Veröffentlichung. Nach Edwards erschien eine Oktavausgabe 'erst fünf Jahre später' (1852). Sie wurde hier nur verwendet, wenn Unstimmigkeiten zwischen den drei anderen Quellen auftraten.

Die ersten drei Ausgaben, die unter Mendelssohns Anleitungen zusammengestellt wurden, bilden die Grundlage der vorliegenden Ausgabe. Alle Unterschiede im Gesangsteil werden wiedergegeben. In den Fällen, wo sie zu dem unterliegenden englischen Text in Verbindung stehen, gilt in der Regel, daß die englische Publikation Vorrang hat; dennoch gibt es einige Fälle, in denen Simrocks vollständige Partitur eindeutig vorzuziehen ist. Die Zeichensetzung erfolgt nicht konsequent, sogar nicht im deutschen Text der zwei Simrock Fassungen. Die Vokalausgaben wurden als Ausgangspunkt genommen; wo Markierungen inkonsequent sind oder ganz zu fehlen scheinen, wurden sie mit Hilfe der Gesamtausgabe sowie gelegentlich der Oktavausgabe von Ewer ergänzt. Markierungen wurden nur dann ergänzt, wenn sie in einer der soeben erwähnten Quellen vorkamen. Die Begleitung in den Ausgaben von Simrock und Ewer ist fast identisch; dies kann wohl niemanden überraschen, da es sich hier ja um Mendelssohns eigene Anordnungen handelt. In den wenigen Fällen von Unstimmigkeiten, wurde die vollständige Partitur als maßgebender Faktor benutzt. Bei Simrock finden sich mehr Markierungen, die die Dynamik betreffen. Normal gedruckte Satz- und Dynamikmarkierungen in der vorliegenden Ausgabe, erscheinen in den Klavierausgaben und der vollständigen Fassung. Kleingedruckte dynamische Zeichen und Satzmarkierungen mit durchgestrichenen Linien erscheinen nur in den Klavierausgaben, nicht jedoch in der Gesamtausgabe; eckige Klammern enthalten nur Markierungen aus der vollständigen Ausgabe. Metronombezeichnungen finden sich in der Gesamtausgabe, dem Ewer Oktavband, und nur im zweiten Teil der Ewer Folioausgabe; sie stimmen durchweg überein. Durch Noten und Ossia verweist 'Simrock' auf die Gesamtausgabe, 'Simrock VS' auf die deutsche Gesangsausgabe; 'Ewer' auf die erste Folioausgabe von 1847, und 'Ewer 1852' auf die Oktavausgabe, zu der Unterschiede bestehen. Die Libretti wurden wie in den ursprünglichen Ausgaben gedruckt, mit Ausnahme einiger biblischer Hinweise. Simrocks Gesamt- und Vokalausgabe enthalten dasselbe (deutsche) Libretto; weder dieses noch das englische Libretto von Ewer stimmen völlig mit den Worten überein, wie sie in der Musik stehen.

Die jüngst Novello Vokalausgabe stammt von 1903 und hat einen anonymen Redakteur. Sie beansprucht, mit der Gesamtausgabe, die von Professor Julius Rietz als ein Teil der Mendelssohn Werke: Kritische durchgesehene Ausgabe (herausgegeben von Breitkopf und Härtel, 1874-77) bearbeitet worden war, übereinzustimmen. Es ist jedoch offensichtlich, daß letztere nur auf der Gesamtausgabe basierte, und Professor Rietz dazu neigte, Unstimmigkeiten in der Phrasierung ohne Kommentar zu beseitigen. Die Ausgabe von 1903 bedient sich in vielen Fällen der deutschen Noten und Rhythmen des Originals, paßt die englische Unterlage diesem an, und macht damit Mendelssohns sorgfältige Anweisungen, die oben beschrieben wurden, zunichte. Die Begleitung wurde auch überarbeitet; sie enthält mehr Orchesterteile als Mendelssohn für zwei Hände für machbar hielt.

Obwohl das vorliegende Werk 42 Teile enthält, sollten nur wenige Pausen eingelegt werden. Teile 1-5 sowie 6-9 gefolgt von 10-17 sind fortlaufend. 18 scheint als Zwischenspiel angelegt zu sein bevor 19-20 den ersten Teil abschließen. 21-22 bilden die Einleitung zum zweiten Teil. 23-29 sowie 30 bis zum Ende sind fortlaufend, abgesehen von einer kurzen Pause zwischen 39 und 40. Einige andere Pausen wären möglich, sind jedoch nicht zu empfehlen. Mendelssohns Hauptinteresse galt dem dramatischen Effekt dieses Werks. Jede unnötige Pause schwächt die Dramatik.

Michael Pilkington, Old Coulsdon, 1991

Der Hauptteil der Information in diesem Vorwort entstammt 'The History of Mendelssohn's Oratorio "Elijah" ', von F.G. Edwards. Novello, Ewer and Co., 1896. Auf 130 Seiten werden die Entstehung von *Elias*, die erste Aufführung sowie spätere Überarbeitungen beschrieben. Edwards verwendete die folgenden Quellen:

1. Briefe an Karl Klingemann, die ihm von Dr. Carl Klingemann und Dr. Felix Klingemann geliehen wurden.

2. Briefwechsel zwischen Felix Mendelssohn Bartholdy und Julius Schubring, zugleich ein Beitrag zur Geschichte und Theorie des Oratoriums. Herausgegeben von Prof. Dr. Jul. Schubring, Direktor des Katharineums zu Lübeck. Leipzig: Verlag von Duncker und Humblot. 1892.

3. Briefe von Felix Mendelssohn Bartholdy, 1833-1847. Herausgegeben von Paul Mendelssohn Bartholdy und Dr Carl Mendelssohn Bartholdy. 1863.

4. Briefe an Joseph Moore, Manager des Birmingham Festivals von 1802 bis zu seinem Tod 1851, geschrieben auf Englisch; Leihgabe von William Moore an F.G. Edwards.

5. F.G. Edwards zitiert so als ob ihm jemand dieses erzählt hat.

6. Memoir of Madame Jenny Lind-Goldschmidt. H. Scott Holland and W.S. Rockstro. John Murray. 1891.

7. 'Ich bringe Frau Victor Benecke (Mendelssohns ältester Tochter) meinen besten Dank dafür zum Ausdruck, daß sie mir half, die Erlaubnis zu bekommen, zahlreiche bisher unveröffentlichte Briefe, die sich auf den "Elias" beziehen, veröffentlichen zu dürfen.' F.G. Edwards.

8. Briefe Mendelssohns an I. und C. Moscheles. Felix Moscheles. Trübner. Leipzig, 1888.

9. Fräulein Elizabeth Mounsey, die Schwägerin William Bartholomews, half F.G. Edwards, in den Besitz von vierzehn englischen Originalbriefen Mendelssohns an seinen Übersetzer zu kommen.

10. 'Ich bin Frau Geheimrath Wach aus Leipzig (Mendelssohns jüngster Tochter) und ihrer Tochter sehr dankbar dafür, daß sie so freundlich waren und die lange Korrespondenz zwischen Bartholomew und Mendelssohn bezüglich des "Elias" kopierten.' F.G. Edwards.

Libretto, wie zu Anfang der Simrock Ausgabe. Details in eckigen Klammern [ ] erscheinen nur im Hauptteil der Partitur. Angaben in Kursivdruck erscheinen nicht im Hauptteil der Partitur.

ELIAS
Ein Oratorium
nach Worten des alten Testaments

ERSTER THEIL

Einleitung

Elias   So wahr der Herr, der Gott Israels, lebt, vor dem ich stehe: Es soll diese Jahre weder Thau noch Regen kommen, ich sage es denn. [1 Kön. 17: 1]

[No. 1] Chor

(Das Volk)   Hilf, Herr! willst du uns denn gar vertilgen? Die Ernte ist vergangen, der Sommer ist dahin! und uns ist keiner zu Hülfe gekommen! [Jer. 8: 20] Will denn der Herr nicht mehr Gott sein in Zion? [Jer. 8:19]

Chor-Recitativ (Das Volk)   Die Tiefe ist versieget, und die Ströme sind vertrocknet; dem Säugling klebt die Zunge am Gaumen vor Durst! die jungen Kinder heischen Brod; und da ist Niemand, der es ihnen breche! [Klagl. 4:4]

[No. 2] Duett *und* [**mit**] **Chor** (Das Volk)
Chor   Herr, höre unser Gebet! [Ps. 55:1]
(Zwei Stimmen)   Zion streckt ihre Hände aus, und da ist Niemand der sie tröste. [Klagl. 1:17]

[No. 3] *Recitativ* [**Recitativo**]

(Obadja) [Obadjah]   Zerreisset eure Herzen, und nicht eure Kleider! um unsrer Sünden willen hat Elias den Himmel verschlossen, durch das Wort des Herrn! So bekehret euch zu dem Herrn, eurem Gott, denn er ist gnädig, barmherzig, geduldig und von grosser Güte und reut ihn bald der Strafe. [Joel 2:13]

[No. 4] *Arie* [**Aria**]

(Obadja)   'So ihr mich von ganzem Herzen suchet, so will ich mich finden lassen', spricht unser Gott. [Jer. 29:13,14] Ach! dass ich wüsste, wie ich ihn finden, und zu seinem Stuhle kommen möchte! [Hiob 23:3]

[No. 5] Chor

(Das Volk)   Aber der Herr sieht es nicht, er spottet unser! Der Fluch ist über uns gekommen, er wird uns verfolgen bis er uns tödtet. [5 Mose 28:15, 22] 'Denn ich der Herr dein Gott, [ich] bin ein eifriger Gott, der da heimsucht der Väter Missethat an den Kindern bis ins dritte und vierte Glied derer die mich hassen.

Und thue Barmherzigkeit an vielen Tausenden, die mich lieb haben und meine Gebote halten.' [2 Mose 20:5, 6]

[No. 6] Recitativ

(Der Engel) [Ein Engel]   Elias! gehe weg von hinnen, und wende dich gen Morgen, und verbirg dich am Bache Crith! Du sollst vom Bache trinken, und die Raben werden dir Brot bringen des Morgens und des Abends, nach dem Wort deines Gottes. [1 Kön. 17:3,4,6]

[No. 7] Doppel-Quartett

(Die Engel)   Denn er hat seinen Engeln befohlen über dir, dass sie dich behüten auf allen deinen Wegen, dass sie dich auf den Händen tragen, und du deinen Fuss nicht an einen Stein stossest. [Ps. 91:11, 12]

Recitativ

(Der Engel) [Ein Engel]   Nun auch der Bach vertrocknet ist, Elias, mache dich auf, gehe gen Zarpath und bleibe daselbst! Denn der Herr hat daselbst einer Wittwe geboten, dass sie dich versorge. Das Mehl im Cad soll nicht verzehret werden, und dem Oelkruge soll nichts mangeln, bis auf den Tag, da der Herr regnen lassen wird auf Erden. [1 Kön. 17:7,9,14]

[No. 8] [Aria]

(Die Wittwe)   Was hast du an mir gethan, du Mann Gottes? Du bist zu mir hereingekommen, dass meiner Missethat gedacht und mein Sohn getödtet werde! Hilf mir, du Mann Gottes! mein Sohn ist krank, und seine Krankheit ist so hart, dass kein Odem mehr in ihm bleib. [1 Kön. 17:18,17] Ich netze mit meinen Thränen mein Lager die ganze Nacht; [Ps. 6:7] du schaust das Elend, sei du der Armen Helfer. [Ps. 10:14] Hilf meinem Sohn! Es ist kein Odem mehr in ihm.

(Elias)   Gib mir her deinen Sohn! [1 Kön. 17:19] Herr, mein Gott, vernimm mein Wort [Fleh'n], wende dich, Herr, und sei ihr gnädig! und hilf dem Sohne deiner Magd! Denn du bist gnädig, barmherzig, geduldig und von grosser Güte und Treue. [Ps. 86:16,15] Herr, mein Gott, lasse die Seele dieses Kindes wieder zu ihm kommen! [1 Kön. 17:21]

(DIE WITTWE) Wirst du denn unter den Todten Wunder thun? [Ps. 88:11] Es ist kein Odem mehr in ihm! [1 Kön. 17:17]

(ELIAS) Herr, mein Gott, lasse die Seele dieses Kindes wieder zu ihm kommen!

(DIE WITTWE) Werden die Gestorbnen aufsteh'n und dir danken? [Ps. 88:11]

(ELIAS) Herr, mein Gott, Lasse die Seele dieses Kindes wieder zu ihm kommen!

(DIE WITTWE) Der Herr erhört deine Stimme, die Seele des Kindes kommt wieder! Es wird lebendig! [1 Kön. 17:22]

(ELIAS) Siehe da, dein Sohn lebet! [1 Kön. 17:23]

(DIE WITTWE) Nun erkenne ich, dass du ein Mann Gottes bist, und des Herrn Wort in deinem Munde ist Wahrheit! [1 Kön. 17:24] Wie soll ich dem Herrn vergelten alle seine Wohlthat, die er an mir thut? [Ps. 116:12]

(ELIAS) Du sollst den Herrn deinen Gott lieb haben von ganzem Herzen, von ganzer Seele, von allem Vermögen. [5 Mose 6:5] Wohl dem, der den Herrn fürchtet! [Ps. 112:1]

[No. 9] Chor

Wohl dem, der den Herrn fürchtet, und auf seinen Wegen geht! [Den Frommen geht das Licht auf in der Finsterniss.] Den Frommen geht das Licht auf von dem Gnädigen, Barmherzigen und Gerechten. [Ps. 112:1,4]

[No.10] Recitativ

(ELIAS) So wahr der Herr Zebaoth lebet vor dem ich stehe: Heute im dritten Jahre will ich mich dem Könige zeigen, und der Herr wird wieder regnen lassen auf Erden. [1 Kön. 18:15,1]

(Der König) [AHAB] Bist du's, Elias, bist du's der Israel verwirrt? [1 Kön. 18:17]

(DAS VOLK) Du bist's, Elias, du bist's, der Israel verwirrt!

(ELIAS) Ich verwirre Israel nicht, sondern du, König, und deines Vaters Haus, damit dass ihr des Herrn Gebot verlasst, und wandelt Baalim nach. Wohlan! so sende nun hin, und versammle zu mir das ganze Israel auf den Berg Carmel, und alle Propheten Baals, und alle Propheten des Hains, die vom Tische der Königinn essen: [1 Kön. 18:18,19] da wollen wir sehn, ob Gott der Herr ist.

(Das Volk) Da wollen wir sehn, ob Gott der Herr ist.

(ELIAS) Auf denn, ihr Propheten Baals, erwählet einen Farren und legt kein Feuer daran, und rufet Ihr an den Namen eures Gottes, und ich will den Namen des Herrn anrufen; welcher Gott nun mit Feuer antworten wird, der sei Gott. [1 Kön. 18:25,24]

(Das Volk) Ja, welcher Gott nun mit Feuer antworten wird, der sei Gott.

(ELIAS) Ruft euren Gott zuerst, denn eurer sind viele! Ich aber bin allein übergeblieben, ein Prophet des Herrn. [1 Kön. 18:25,21] Ruft eure Feldgötter, und eure Berggötter!

[No. 11] Chor

(Die Baalspriester) Baal, erhöre uns! [1 Kön. 18:26] Wende dich zu unserm Opfer! Höre uns, mächtiger Gott! Send' uns dein Feuer und vertilge den Feind!

[No. 12] Recitativ [Recitativo und Chor]

(ELIAS) Rufet lauter! Denn er ist ja Gott! Er dichtet, oder er hat zu schaffen, oder ist über Feld, – Oder schläft er vielleicht, dass er aufwache. Rufet lauter! [1 Kön. 18:27]

Chor

(Die Baalspriester) Baal, erhöre uns! Wache auf! warum schläfst du? –

[No. 13] Recitativ [Recitativo und Chor]

(ELIAS) Rufet lauter! Er hört euch nicht! Ritzt euch mit Messern und mit Pfriemen nach eurer Weise! Hinkt um den Altar, den ihr gemacht, rufet und weissagt! Da wird keine Stimme sein, keine Antwort, kein Aufmerken. [1 Kön. 18:28,26,29]

Chor

(Die Baalspriester) [Baal!] Gieb uns Antwort, Baal! Siehe, die Feinde verspotten uns! Gieb uns Antwort! Gieb uns Antwort!

Arie

(ELIAS) Kommt her, alles Volk, kommt her zu mir! [1 Kön. 18:30]

[No. 14]

Herr Gott Abrahams, Isaaks und Israels, lass heut kund werden, dass du Gott bist und ich dein Knecht, und dass ich solches alles nach deinem Worte gethan! Erhöre mich Herr, erhöre mich, dass dies Volk wisse, dass du, Herr, Gott bist, dass du ihr Herz danach bekehrest! [1 Kön. 18:36,37]

[No. 15]

(Vier Stimmen) Wirf dein Anliegen auf den Herrn, der wird dich versorgen und wird den Gerechten nicht ewiglich in Unruhe lassen. [Ps. 55:23] Denn seine Gnade reicht so weit der Himmel ist, [Ps. 108:5] und keiner wird zu Schanden, der seiner harret. [Ps.25:3]

[No. 16] Recitativ [Recit: und Chor]

(ELIAS) Der du deine Diener machst zu Geistern, und deine Engel zu Feuerflammen, sende sie herab! [Ps. 104:4]

Chor

(DAS VOLK) Das Feuer fiel herab! Die Flamme frass das Brandopfer! Fallt nieder auf euer Angesicht! Der Herr ist Gott, der Herr ist Gott! [1 Kön. 18:38,39] Der Herr unser Gott ist ein einiger Herr [5 Mose 6:4] und es sind keine andern Götter neben ihm. [2 Mose 20:3]

Recitativ

(*Elias und das Volk*) Greift die Propheten Baals, dass ihrer keiner entrinne! Führt sie hinab an den Bach, und schlachtet sie daselbst! [1 Kön. 18:40]

[No. 17] Arie

(ELIAS) Ist nicht des Herrn Wort wie ein Feuer, und wie ein Hammer der Felsen zerschlägt? [Jer. 23:29] [Sein Wort ist wie ein Feuer, und wie ein Hammer, der Felsen zerschlägt.] Gott ist ein rechter Richter, und ein Gott der täglich droht; Will man sich nicht bekehren, so hat er sein Schwert gewetzt, und seinen Bogen gespannt und zielet! [Ps. 7:12,13]

[No. 18] [Arioso]

Eine Stimme Weh ihnen, dass sie von mir weichen! Sie müssen zerstöret werden, denn sie sind abtrünnig von mir geworden! Ich wollte sie wohl erlösen, wenn sie nicht Lügen wider mich lehrten. [Hos. 7:13] [Ich wollte sie wohl erlösen, sie hören es nicht.]

[No. 19] *Recitativ* [Recit: und Chor]

(*Obadja*) [OBADJAH] Hilf deinem Volk, du Mann Gottes! Es ist doch ja unter der Heiden Götzen keiner, der Regen könnte geben; so kann der Himmel auch nicht regnen; denn Gott allein kann solches alles thun. [Jer. 14:22]

(ELIAS) O Herr! du hast nun deine Feinde verworfen und zerschlagen! So schaue nun vom Himmel herab, und wende die Noth deines Volkes; öffne den Himmel und fahre herab. Hilf deinem Knecht, o du mein Gott. [2 Chron. 6:24]

[Chor]

(*Das Volk*) Öffne den Himmel und fahre herab! Hilf deinem Knecht, o du mein Gott.

(ELIAS) Gehe hinauf, Knabe, und schaue zum Meere zu, [1 Kön. 18:43] ob der Herr mein Gebet erhört?

(DER KNABE) Ich sehe nichts! Der Himmel ist ehern über meinem Haupte. [5 Mose 28:23]

(ELIAS) Wenn der Himmel verschlossen wird, weil sie an dir gesündiget haben, und sie werden beten und deinen Namen bekennen und sich von ihren Sünden bekehren, so wollest du ihnen gnädig sein. [Hilf deinem Knecht, o du mein Gott!] [2 Chron. 6:26,27]

(*Das Volk*) So wollest du uns gnädig sein! Hilf deinem Knecht, o du mein Gott!

(ELIAS) Gehe wieder hin und schaue zum Meere zu. [1 Kön. 18:43]

(DER KNABE) Ich sehe nichts! Die Erde ist eisern unter mir. [5 Mose 28:23]

(ELIAS) Rauscht es nicht, als wollte es regnen? [1 Kön. 18:41] Siehest du noch nichts vom Meere her?

(DER KNABE) Ich sehe nichts!

(ELIAS) Wende dich zum Gebet deines Knechts, zu seinem Flehn, [2 Chron. 6:19] Herr du mein Gott! Wenn ich rufe zu dir, Herr mein Hort, so schweige mir nicht! [Ps. 28:1] Gedenke Herr an deine Barmherzigkeit!

(DER KNABE) Es gehet eine kleine Wolke auf aus dem Meere, wie eines Mannes Hand. Der Himmel wird schwarz von Wolken und Wind; es rauschet stärker und stärker! [1 Kön. 18:44,45]

(*Das Volk*) Danket dem Herrn, denn er ist freundlich.

(ELIAS) Danket dem Herrn, denn er ist freundlich, und seine Güte währet ewiglich. [Ps. 106:1]

[No. 20] [Chor]

Dank sei dir Gott, du tränkest [*oder* tränk'st] das durst'ge Land! Die Wasserströme erheben sich, sie erheben ihr Brausen, die Wasserwogen sind gross, und brausen gewaltig; doch der Herr ist noch grösser in der Höhe. [Ps. 93:3,4]

ZWEITER THEIL

[No. 21] Arie

(*Eine Stimme*) Höre, Israel, höre des Herrn Stimme! Ach, dass du merktest auf sein Gebot! Aber wer glaubt unsrer Predigt, und wem wird der Arm des Herrn geoffenbart? So spricht der Herr, der Erlöser Israels, sein Heiliger zum Knecht der unter den Tyrannen ist: [so spricht der Herr] Ich, Ich bin euer Tröster. Weiche nicht, denn ich bin dein Gott, ich stärke dich! Wer bist du denn? dass du dich vor Menschen fürchtest, die doch sterben und vergissest des Herrn, der dich gemacht hat, *und* [der] den Himmel ausbreitet und die Erde gründet. [Jes. 48:18;53:1;49:7;41:10; 51:12,13]

[No. 22] Chor

Fürchte dich nicht, spricht unser Gott; fürchte dich nicht, ich bin mit dir, ich helfe dir. [Jes. 41:10] [dein Gott, der zu dir spricht: Fürchte dich nicht!] Ob tausend fallen zu deiner Seite und zehentausend zu deiner Rechten, so wird es doch dich nicht treffen. [Ps. 91:7]

[No. 23] *Recitativ* [**Recitativo und Chor**]

(ELIAS) Der Herr hat dich erhoben aus dem Volk, und dich zum König über Israel gesetzt; aber du, Ahab, hast uebel gethan über alle die vor dir gewesen sind. Es war dir ein Geringes, dass du wandeltest in der Sünde Jerobeam's, und machtest dem Baal einen Hain, den Herrn den Gott Israels, zu erzürnen. Du hast todt geschlagen, und fremdes Gut genommen! Und der Herr wird Israel schlagen, wie ein Rohr im Wasser bewegt wird, und wird Israel übergeben um eurer Sünde willen! [1 Kön. 14:7,9;16:31, 32,33; 21:19;14:15,16]

(Die Königinn)

[DIE KÖNIGIN] Habt ihr's gehört, wie er geweissagt hat wider dieses Volk? [Jer. 26:9]

(Das Volk) Wir haben es gehört!

(DIE KÖNIGINN) Wie er geweissagt hat wider den König in Israel?

(Das Volk) Wir haben es gehört!

(DIE KÖNIGINN) Warum darf er weissagen im Namen des Herrn? Was wäre für ein Königreich in Israel, [Jer. 26:8] wenn Elias Macht hätte über des Königs Macht? Die Götter thun mir dies und das, wenn ich nicht morgen um diese Zeit seiner Seele thue, wie dieser Seelen einer. [1 Kön. 21:7] die er geopfert hat am Bache Kison. –

(Das Volk) Er muss sterben! [Jer. 26:8]

(Die Königinn und das Volk) Er hat die Propheten Baals getödtet; er hat sie mit dem Schwerte erwürgt; er hat den Himmel verschlossen, er hat die theure Zeit über uns gebracht! [Sirach 48:3,2] so ziehet hin und greift Elias, er ist des Todes schuldig, [Jer. 26:11] tödtet ihn, lasst uns ihm thun wie er gethan hat!

[No. 24] **Chor**

(Das Volk) Wehe ihm! er muss sterben! Warum darf er den Himmel verschliessen? Warum darf er weissagen im Namen des Herrn? Dieser ist des Todes schuldig, denn er hat geweissagt wider diese Stadt, wie wir mit unsern Ohren gehört. Dieser ist des Todes schuldig, so ziehet hin, greifet ihn, tödtet ihn!

[No. 25] **Recitativ**

(Obadja) Du Mann Gottes, lass meine Rede etwas vor dir gelten! [2 Kön. 1:13] So spricht die Königinn: Elias ist des Todes schuldig; und sie sammeln sich wider dich, sie stellen deinem Gange Netze, [Ps. 59:4;57:7] und ziehen aus, dass sie dich greifen, dass sie dich tödten! So mache dich auf, und wende dich von ihnen, gehe hin in die Wüste! Der Herr,

dein Gott wird selber mit dir wandeln; er wird die Hand nicht abthun, noch dich verlassen, [5 Mose 31:6] Ziehe hin, und segne uns auch! [2 Mose 12:32]

(ELIAS) Sie wollen sich nicht bekehren! [Jer. 5:3] Bleibe hier du Knabe; der Herr sei mit euch! Ich gehe hin in die Wüste! [1 Kön. 19:4]

[No. 26] **Arie**

(ELIAS) Es ist genug! So nimm nun, Herr, meine Seele; ich bin nicht besser, denn meine Väter. [1 Kön. 19:4] Ich begehre nicht mehr zu leben, denn meine Tage sind vergeblich gewesen; [Hiob 7:16] ich habe geeifert um den Herrn, [um] den Gott Zebaoth, denn die Kinder Israels haben deinen Bund verlassen, und deine Altäre haben sie zerbrochen, und deine Propheten mit dem Schwert erwürgt. Und ich bin allein übrig geblieben, und sie *stehen* [steh'n] danach, dass sie mir mein Leben nehmen! [1 Kön. 19:10] Es ist genug! So nimm nun, Herr, meine Seele!

[No. 27] **Recitativ**

(Eine Stimme) Siehe, er schläft unter dem Wacholder in der Wüste! [1 Kön. 19:4] Aber die Engel des Herrn lagern sich um die her, so ihn fürchten. [Ps. 34:8]

[No. 28] *Terzett* [**Terzetto**]

(DIE ENGEL) Hebe deine Augen auf zu den Bergen von welchen dir Hülfe kommt! Deine Hülfe kommt vom Herrn, der Himmel und Erde gemacht hat. Er wird deinen Fuss nicht gleiten lassen, und der dich behütet, schläft nicht. [Ps. 121:1,2,3]

[No. 29] **Chor**

Siehe der Hüter Israel's schläft noch schlummert nicht; wenn du mitten in Angst wandelst, so erquickt er dich. [Ps. 121:4;138:7]

[No. 30] **Recitativ**

(DER ENGEL) Stehe auf Elias, denn du hast einen grossen Weg vor dir! Vierzig Tage und vierzig Nächte sollst du gehen [geh'n] bis an den Berg Gottes Horeb. [1 Kön. 19:7,8]

(ELIAS) O Herr, ich arbeite vergeblich, und bringe meine Kraft umsonst und unnütz zu! Ach dass du den Himmel zerrissest und führest herab! Dass die Berge vor dir zerflössen! Dass deine Feinde vor dir zittern müssten, durch die Wunder die du thust! Warum lässest du sie irren von deinen Wegen, und ihr Herz verstocken, dass sie dich nicht fürchten? O, dass meine Seele stürbe! [Jes. 49:4;64:1,2,3; 63:17]

[No. 31] **Arie**

(DER ENGEL) Sei stille dem Herrn, und

warte auf ihn, der wird dir geben, was dein Herz wünscht, Befiehl ihm deine Wege und hoffe auf ihn, stehe ab vom Zorn und lass den Grimm. [Ps. 37:7,4,5,8]

[No. 32] Chor
Wer bis an das Ende beharrt, der wird *seelig* [selig]. [Matth. 10:22]

[No. 33] [Recitativo]
(ELIAS) Herr, es wird Nacht um mich; sei du nicht ferne! Verbirg dein Antlitz nicht vor mir; meine Seele dürstet nach dir, wie ein dürres Land! [Ps. 22:20; 143:7,6]

Recitativ
(DER ENGEL) Wohlan denn, gehe hinaus, und tritt auf den Berg vor den Herrn, denn seine Herrlichkeit erscheinet über dir! Verhülle dein Antlitz, denn es naht der Herr! [1 Kön. 19:11,13]

[No. 34] Chor
Der Herr ging vorüber!
Und ein starker Wind, der die Berge zerriss und die Felsen zerbrach ging vor dem Herrn her. Aber der Herr war nicht im Sturmwind.
Der Herr ging vorüber! Und die Erde erbebte, und das Meer erbrausste. Aber der Herr war nicht im Erdbeben. [1 Kön. 19:11]
Und nach dem Erdbeben kam ein Feuer, [die Erde erbebte, das Meer erbrauste, aber der Herr war nicht im Feuer.] und nach dem Feuer kam ein stilles, sanftes Sausen. [1 Kön. 19:12]
Und in dem Säuseln nahte sich der Herr.

[No. 35] Solo und Chor [Recitativo]
Seraphim standen über ihm, und einer rief zum andern:

[Quartett mit Chor]
Heilig, heilig, heilig ist Gott der Herr. [der Herr Zebaoth.] Alle Lande sind seiner Ehre voll. [Jes. 6:2,3]

[No. 36] Chor-Recitativ
Gehe wiederum hinab, noch sind übrig geblieben siebentausend in Israel, die sich nicht gebeugt vor Baal. [1 Kön. 19:15,18] Gehe wiederum hinab! Thue nach des Herrn Wort!
(ELIAS) Ich gehe hinab in der Kraft des Herrn! Du bist ja der Herr! ich muss um deinetwillen leiden; darum freuet sich mein Herz und ich bin fröhlich; auch mein Fleisch wird sicher liegen. [Ps. 71:16;16:2]

[No. 37] Arioso
(ELIAS) Ja es sollen wohl Berge weichen und Hügel hinfallen, aber deine Gnade wird nicht von mir weichen, und der Bund deines Friedens soll nicht fallen! [Jes. 54:10]

[No. 38] Chor
Und der Prophet Elias brach hervor wie ein Feuer, und sein Wort brannte wie eine Fackel. Er hat stolze Könige gestürzt; er hat auf dem Berge Sinai gehört die zukünftige Strafe und in Horeb die Rache. [Sirach 48:1,6,7]
Und da der Herr ihn wollte gen Himmel holen, siehe da kam ein feuriger Wagen mit feurigen Rossen, und er fuhr im Wetter gen Himmel. [2 Kön. 2:1,11]

[No. 39] Arie
Dann werden die Gerechten leuchten, wie die Sonne in ihres Vaters Reich. [Matth 13:43] Wonne und Freude werden sie ergreifen, aber Trauern und Seufzen wird vor ihnen fliehen. [Jes. 51:11]

[No. 40]
Eine Stimme Darum ward gesendet der Prophet Elias, eh' denn da komme der grosse und schreckliche Tag des Herrn; er soll das Herz der Väter bekehren zu den Kindern, und das Herz der Kinder zu ihren Vätern, dass der Herr nicht komme und das Erdreich mit dem Banne schlage! [Mal. 3:23,24]

[No. 41] Chor
Aber einer erwacht von Mitternacht, und er kommt vom Aufgang der Sonne; der wird des Herrn Namen predigen und wird über die Gewaltigen gehen; das ist sein Knecht, sein Auserwählter, an welchem seine Seele Wohlgefallen hat! Auf ihm wird ruhen der Geist des Herrn; der Geist der Weisheit und des Verstandes, der Geist des Raths und der Stärke, der Geist der Erkenntniss und der Furcht des Herrn. [Jes. 41:25; 42:1;11:2]

[Quartetto]
Vier Stimmen Wohlan, alle die ihr durstig seid, kommt her zum Wasser, kommt her zu ihm! [und] Neigt euer Ohr und kommt zu ihm, so wird eure Seele leben. [Jes. 55:1,3]

[No. 42] Schluss-Chor
Alsdann wird euer Licht hervorbrechen, wie die Morgenröthe, und eure Besserung wird schnell wachsen, und die Herrlichkeit des Herrn wird Euch zu sich nehmen. [Jes. 58:8]
Herr unser Herrscher, wie herrlich ist dein Name in allen Landen, da man dir danket im Himmel. [Ps. 8:2] Amen.

FIRST PART   *ERSTER THEIL*

Introduction   *Einleitung*

Grave ♩ = 60

ELIJAH (Bass)
ELIAS p

As God the Lord of Is - ra - el liv - eth, be - fore__
So wahr der Herr, der Gott I - sra - els, le - bet, vor dem ich

whom I stand; there shall not be dew nor rain these years, there shall not be
ste - he: Es soll die - se Jah - re we - der Thau noch Re - gen

dew nor rain, but ac - cord - ing to my word.
kom - men, ich sa - ge es denn.

Overture   *Ouverture*

Moderato ma poco a poco con più di fuoco ♩ = 92

sempre pp

* ♩ ♩ |♩. ♪ ♩ | (Mendelssohn, 3.7.1846)

years, not dew nor rain,

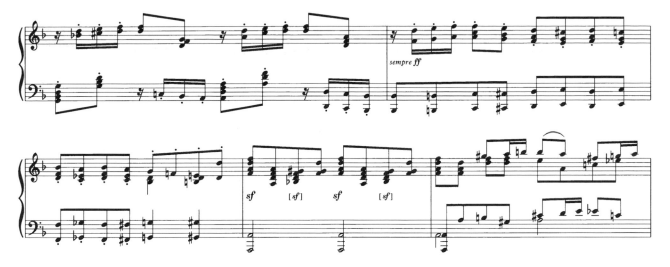

No. 1

Chorus [Help, Lord!]
Chor

8

12

No. 2

Duet with Chorus [Lord! bow Thine ear to our prayer]
Duett mit Chor

*These two Es are not in the orchestral score.

No. 3

Recitative [Ye people, rend your hearts]
Recitativo

Ossia: (suggested alternative to match the sense of the German. M.P.)

gar - ments. For your trans - gres - sions the Pro - phet E - li - jah

No. 4

Aria [If with all your hearts]

Aria

* **Andante tranquillo** (Mendelssohn 3.7.46)

* ♪♪♪♪ |♩♩ (Mendelssohn 3.7.46)
come͜ e-ven to his seat͟
pre-sence

No. 5   Chorus [Yet doth the Lord see it not]
Chor

*Bass: fal-len down up-on us; (Ewer)

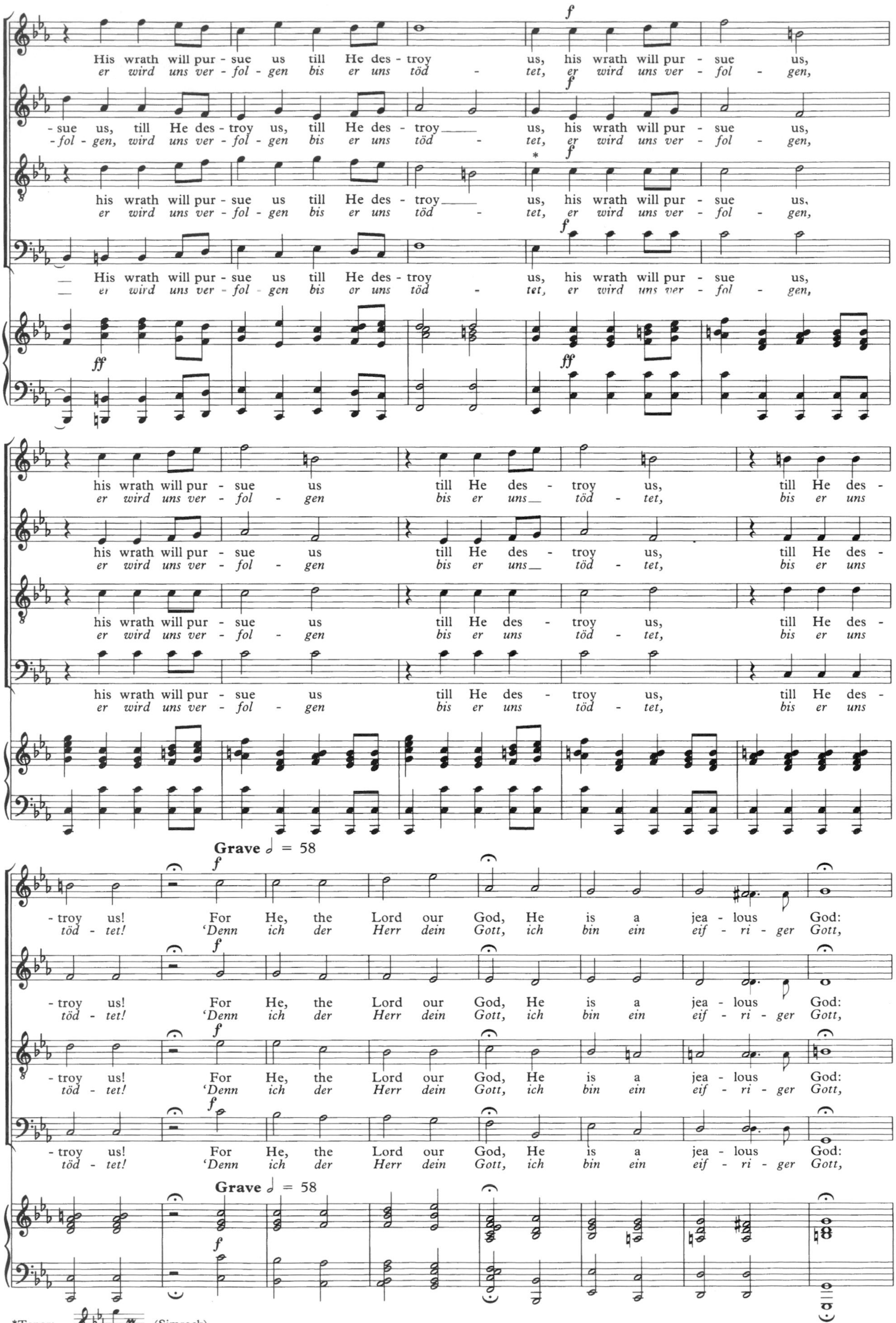

*Tenor: us (Simrock)

and He vis - it - eth all the fa - thers' sins on the chil - dren
der da heim - sucht der Vä - ter Mis - se - that an den Kin - dern,

and He vis - it - eth all the fa - thers' sins on the chil - dren
der da heim - sucht der Vä - ter Mis - se - that an den Kin - dern

and He vis - it - eth all the fa - thers' sins on the chil - dren
der da heim - sucht der Vä - ter Mis - se - that an den Kin - dern,

and He vis - it - eth all the fa - thers' sins on the chil - dren
der da heim - sucht der Vä - ter Mis - se - that an den Kin - dern,

to the third and the fourth gen - er - a - tion of them that hate
bis in's drit - te und vier - te Glied de - rer die mich has -

to the third and the fourth gen - er - a - tion of them that hate
bis in's drit - te und vier - te Glied de - rer die mich has -

to the third and the fourth gen - er - a - tion of them that hate
bis in's drit - te und vier - te Glied de - rer die mich has -

to the third and the fourth gen - er - a - tion of them that hate
bis in's drit - te und vier - te Glied de - rer die mich has -

C

Him. His mer - cies on thou - sands
- sen. Und thu - e Barm - her - zig -

Him. His mer - cies on thou - sands
- sen. Und thu - e Barm - her - zig -

Him. His mer - cies on thou - sands
- sen. Und thu - e Barm - her - zig -

Him. His mer - cies on thou - sands
- sen. Und thu - e Barm - her - zig -

C

*Bass: (Ewer)
fa - thers'

*Alto: -cies on (Ewer)

No. 6 Recitative [Elijah! Get thee hence]
Recitativo

AN ANGEL (Alto)
EIN ENGEL

E - li - jah, get thee hence E - li - jah; de-
E - li - as! ge - he weg von hin - nen und

-part, and turn thee east - ward, thi - ther hide thee by Che-rith's brook.
wen - de dich gen Mor - gen, und ver - birg dich am Ba - che Crith!

There shalt thou drink its wa - ters; and the Lord thy God hath com-mand - ed the
du sollst vom Ba - che trin - ken und die Ra - ben wer - den dir Brod brin - gen des

Tempo Andante Recit.

ra - vens to feed thee there; so do ac-cord-ing un-to his word.____
Mor - gens und des A - bends, nach dem Wort dei - nes Got - tes.

Tempo Andante

Recit.

[p]

attacca No.7

No. 7

Double Quartet (Angels)   *Doppel Quartett (Die Engel)*
[For He shall give his angels charge over thee]

31

*Bass 2: (Simrock)
all the

in all the ways thou go - est;
auf al - len dei - nen We - gen.
in all the ways thou go - est;
auf al - len dei - nen We - gen.
in all the ways thou go - est;
auf al - len dei - nen We - gen.
in all the ways thou go - est;
auf al - len dei - nen We - gen.
ways thou go - est. for He shall give his an - gels charge o - ver
dei - nen We - gen, denn er hat sei - nen En - geln be - fäh - len ü - ber
sf
[p]
sf
cresc.
That their hands shall up-hold and guide thee, that their
Dass sie dich auf den Hän - den tra - gen, dass sie
f
thee; that their hands shall up-hold and guide thee,
dir, dass sie dich auf den Hän - den tra - gen,
cresc.

*Alto 2: 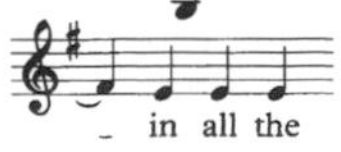 (Ewer, but clearly a misprint)
in all the

33

*Tenor 2: stone____ shall up-

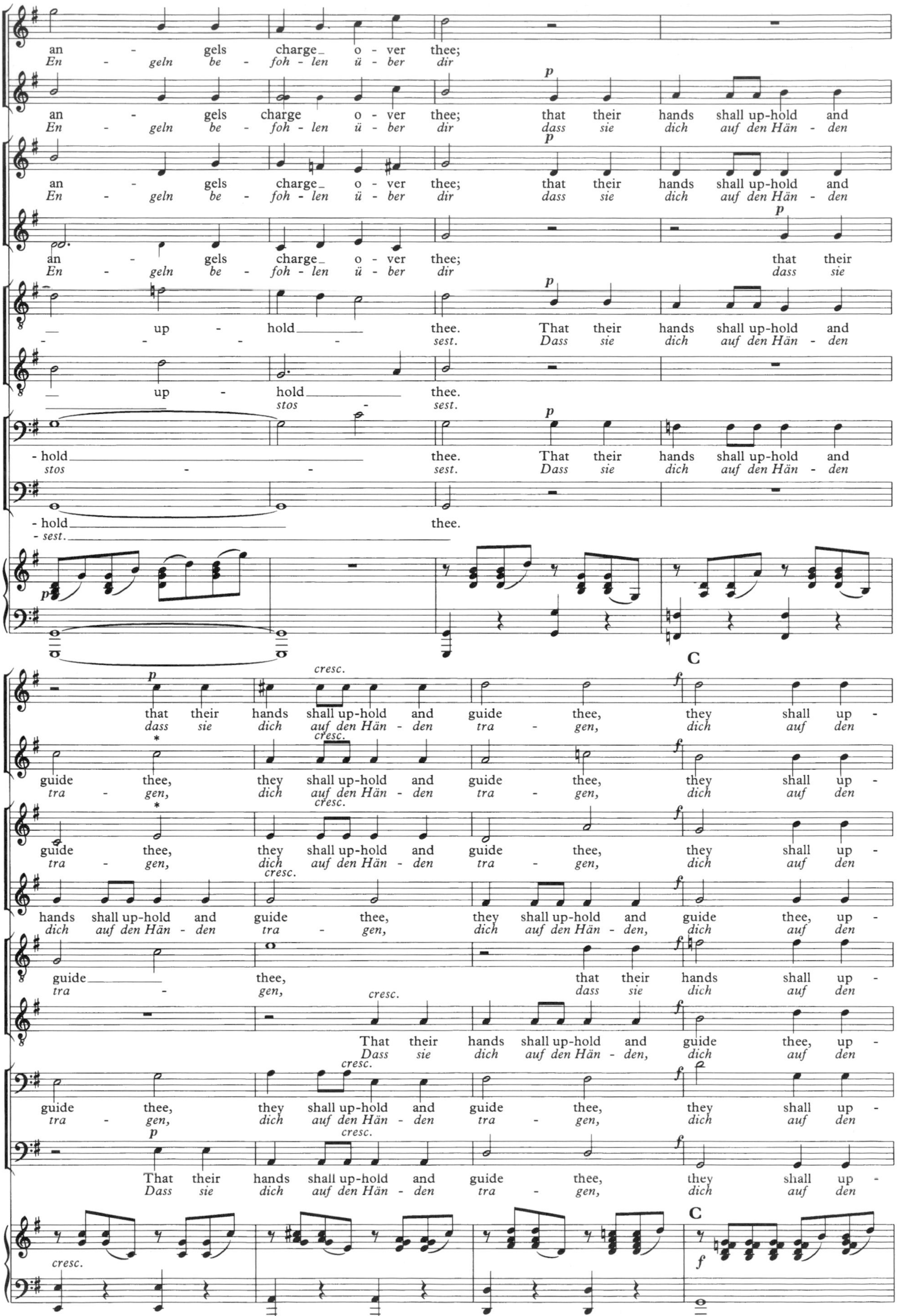

*Sop. 2, Alto 1: thee,___ shall up-hold (Simrock)

Recitative *[Now Cherith's brook is dried up]
[*Recit.*]

THE ANGEL (Alto)
EIN ENGEL

Now Cher-ith's brook is dri-ed up, E-li-jah, a-rise and de-part, and
Nun auch der Bach ver-trock-net ist, E-li-as, ma-che dich auf,

get thee to Za-re-phath, thi-ther a-bide: for the Lord hath com-mand-ed
ge-he gen Zar-path und blei-be da-selbst! denn der Herr hat da-selbst ei-ner

a tempo andante

a wi-dow wo-man there to sus-tain thee; and the bar-rel of meal shall not
Witt-we ge-bo-ten, dass sie dich ver-sor-ge. Das Mehl im Cad soll nicht ver-zeh-ret

waste, nei-ther shall the cruse of oil fail, un-til the
wer-den, und dem Oel-kru-ge soll nichts man-geln bis auf den

Tempo

day that the Lord send-eth rain up-on the earth.
Tag, da der Herr reg-nen las-sen wird auf Er-den.

*Both sources place the heading information above the second bar, with the music running continuously from the previous page.

No. 8

Aria [What have I to do with thee?]*

Aria

THE WIDOW (Soprano)
DIE WITTWE

What have I to do with thee, O man of
Was hast du an mir ge-than, du Mann

God?___ art thou come to me, to call my sin___ un-to re-mem-brance? to slay my
Got-tes? du bist zu mir her-ein ge-kom-men dass mei-ner Mis-se-that ge-dacht, und mein

son art thou come hi-ther? Help me, man of God,___ my son is
Sohn ge-töd-tet wer-de! Hilf mir,___ du Mann Got-tes! mein Sohn ist

sick!   and his sick-ness is so
krank,   und sei-ne Krank-heit ist so

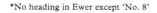

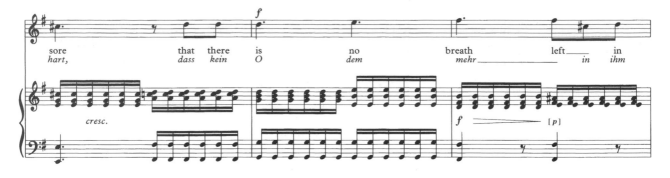

sore that there is no breath left in
hart, dass kein O dem mehr in ihm

him, no breath left, no breath, no
blieb, kein O - dem, kein O - dem

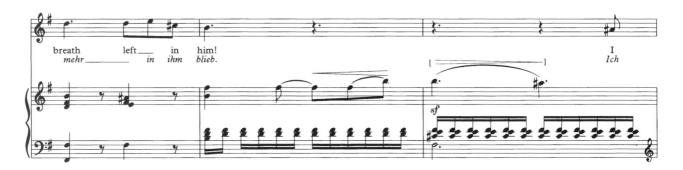

breath left in him! I
mehr in ihm blieb. Ich

A

go mourn-ing all the day long, I lie down and weep at night; I
net - ze mit mei - nen Thrä nen mein La - ger die gan - ze Nacht. Ich

go mourn-ing all the day long, I lie down and weep at
net - ze mit mei nen Thrä nen mein La - ger die gan - ze

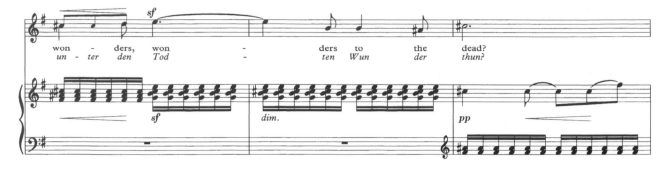

won - ders, won - ders to the dead?
un - ter den Tod - ten Wun - der thun?

sf dim. pp

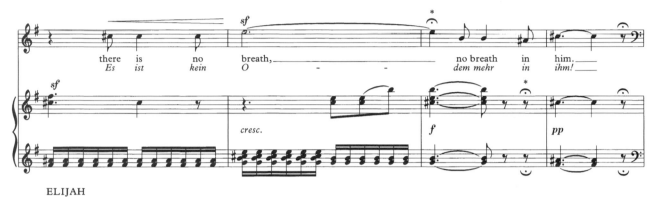

there is no breath, no breath in him.
Es ist kein O - - dem mehr in ihm!

sf cresc. f pp

ELIJAH
ELIAS
cresc. sempre cresc. f

Lord my God, let the spi - rit of this child re - turn, that he a -
Herr, mein Gott, las - se die See - le die - ses Kin - des wie - der zu ihm

p cresc.

THE WIDOW
DIE WITTWE
Recit. sf

- gain may live! Shall the dead a - rise, the dead a - rise and praise Thee?
- kom - men! Wer - den die Ge - storb - nen auf - steh'n und dir dan - ken?

f

D
ELIJAH
ELIAS
Recit. ff

Lord my God, O let the spi - rit of this child re - turn, that he a - gain may
Herr, mein Gott! las - se die See - le die - ses Kin - des wie - der zu ihm kom -

Recit. ff [ ] ff [ ] ff [ ] [pp/p]

*This unusual configuration of fermatas is intended to convey the following: The accompaniment leaves the chord in strict time and waits in silence for the voice to catch up. The voice meanwhile holds the first note ad lib. (till after the chord has stopped) and then completes the bar in time.

THE WIDOW
DIE WITTWE

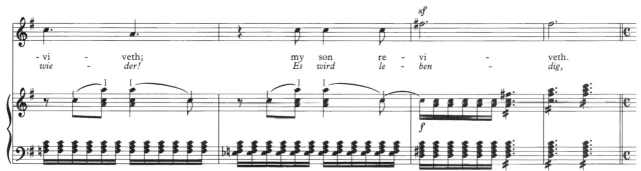

[Segue]

* (Simrock). See Preface for Mendelssohn's comments on the words. † (Simrock)

No.9   Chorus [Blessed are the men who fear Him]
                              Chor

*See Preface for Mendelssohn's comment on the words.

*Sop.: ♩ ♪ (Ewer 1852)   † Bass: ♩ (Ewer 1852)
     ev - er   they

52

*Sop: 𝅘𝅥𝅭 ♪ (Ewer 1852)
der den

No. 10

Recit. with Chorus [As God the Lord]
Recitativo mit Chor

*See Preface for Mendelssohn's comment on the words.

_ have for-sa-ken God's com-mands; and thou hast fol-low'd Baal - im! Now send
- mit dass ihr des Herrn Ge - bot ver - lasst, und wan-delt Baal - im nach. Wohl - an!

and ga - ther to me, send, and ga - ther to me the whole of Is - ra-
so sen - de nun hin, und ver-samm - le zu mir das gan - ze I - sra-

- el un - to Mount Car - mel: There
- el auf den Berg Car - mel! und

sum - mon the pro - phets of Baal, and al - so the pro-phets of the groves who are
al - le Pro-phe - ten Baals, und al - le Pro-phe - ten des Hains, die vom

feast - ed at Je - ze-bel's ta - ble. Then, then we shall see whose God is the
Ti - sche der Kö - ni-ginn es - sen: da wol - len wir seh'n, ob Gott der

*Piano 𝄢 (Ewer) † ? **Andante** 𝅗𝅥 = 72. See Preface.

58

No. 11

Chorus [Baal, we cry to thee]
Chor

A
mf
us! Heed the sac - ri - fice we___ of - fer! Baal,___ O hear us and an - swer us!
uns! Wen - de dich zu un - serm___ O - pfer! Baal,___ er - hö - re, er - hö - re___ uns!
us! Heed the sac - ri - fice we of - fer! Baal,___ O hear us and an - swer us!
uns! Wen - de dich zu un - serm O - pfer! Baal,___ er - hö - re, er - hö - re___ uns!
us! Heed the sac - ri - fice we of - fer! Baal,___ O hear us and an - swer us!
uns! Wen - de dich zu un - serm O - pfer! Baal,___ er - hö - re, er - hö - re uns!
us! Heed the sac - ri - fice we of - fer! Baal,___ O hear us and an - swer us!
uns! Wen - de dich zu un - serm O - pfer! Baal,___ er - hö - re, er - hö - re uns!
us! Baal,___ O hear us and an - swer us! Heed the
uns! Baal,___ er - hö - re, er - hö - re___ uns! Wen - de
us! Baal,___ O hear us and an - swer us! Heed the
uns! Baal,___ er - hö - re, er - hö - re___ uns! Wen - de
us! Baal, O hear us and an - swer us! Heed the
uns! Baal, er - hö - re, er - hö - re uns! Wen - de
us! Baal, O hear us and an - swer us! Heed the
uns! Baal, er - hö - re, er - hö - re uns! Wen - de
A
sf
[f] sf
sf
[mf] f
Baal,___ O hear us and an - swer us! Baal, we cry to thee,
Baal,___ er - hö - re, er - hö - re___ uns! Baal, er - hö - re uns,
Baal,___ O hear us and an - swer us! Baal, we cry to thee,
Baal,___ er - hö - re, er - hö - re___ uns! Baal, er - hö - re uns,
Baal,___ O hear us and an - swer us! Baal, we cry to thee,
Baal,___ er - hö - re, er - hö - re uns! Baal, er - hö - re uns,
Baal,___ O hear us and an - swer us! Baal, we cry to thee,
Baal,___ er - hö - re, er - hö - re uns! Baal, er - hö - re uns,
sac - ri - fice we___ of - fer! Baal,___ O hear us and an - swer us! Baal, we cry to thee, Baal, we
dich zu un - serm___ O - pfer, Baal,___ er - hö - re, er - hö - re___ uns! Baal, er - hö - re uns, Baal, er -
sac - ri - fice we of - fer! Baal, O hear us and an - swer us! Baal, we cry to thee, Baal, we
dich zu un - serm O - pfer, Baal, er - hö - re, er - hö - re___ uns! Baal, er - hö - re uns, Baal, er -
sac - ri - fice we of - fer! Baal,___ O hear us and an - swer us! Baal, we cry to thee, Baal, we
dich zu un - serm O - pfer, Baal,___ er - hö - re, er - hö - re uns! Baal, er - hö - re uns, Baal, er -
sac - ri - fice we of - fer! Baal, O hear us and an - swer us! Baal, we cry to thee, Baal, we
dich zu un - serm O - pfer, Baal, er - hö - re, er - hö - re uns! Baal, er - hö - re uns, Baal, er -
sf
sf
f
sf
sf

*See Preface for Mendelssohn's comment on 'extirpate'.

63

No. 12   Recit. [Call him louder]

Recitativo und Chor

68

Chorus [Hear our cry, O Baal!]
Chorus

No. 13

Recit. [Call him louder]
Recitativo und Chor

Chorus [Baal! Hear and answer]
Chor

*Alto: (Ewer)   †Tenor: (Ewer)

Recitative and Air

No. 14   *Aria*

No. 15   [Quartet: Cast thy burden upon the Lord]
                          [*Vier Stimmen*]

No. 16   Recitative [O Thou, who makest thine Angels, Spirits]
Recit. und Chor

* dotted minim in Score, but with timp. roll ending on beat 3.

† (Simrock)   ** Semibreve rest in Ewer
Let them

*Tenor: Bass: (Simrock)

82

V.S.

attacca subito

No. 17   [Air: Is not his word like a fire?]

* ♩ ♩   (Simrock)

   fire and

ham - mer that break - eth, that break - eth the
Ham - mer, ein Ham - mer, der Fel - sen zer -

rock. His word is like a fire, and like a
- schlägt? sein Wort ist wie ein Feu - er und wie ein

ham - mer, a ham - mer that break - eth the
Ham - mer, ein Ham - mer, der Fel - sen zer -

A

rock. For God is
- schlägt. Gott ist ein

an - gry, an - gry with the wick - ed ev - 'ry day, for
rech - ter Rich - ter, und ein Gott der täg - lich droht; ein

God is an- gry with the wick- ed ev- 'ry day;
rech - ter Rich - ter, und ein Gott der täg - lich droht;

and if the wick- ed turn not; the Lord will whet his
will man sich nicht be - keh ren, so hat er sein Schwert ge -

sword, will whet his sword; and He hath
- wetzt, sein Schwert ge - wetzt, und sei - nen

bent his bow, and made it
Bo - gen ge - spannt, und zie - let,

rea - dy, and made it rea - dy,
zie - let,

* ♩ ♩ ♩ ♩ (Simrock)
Lord will whet his

rea - dy!   Is not his word_____ like a
zie - let!   Ist nicht des Herrn Wort wie ein

B

fire?   and like a
Feu - er?   und wie ein

ham - mer that break - eth the rock, and like a ham - mer that break - eth the
Ham - mer, der Fel - sen zer - schlägt, und wie ein Ham - mer, der Fel - sen zer -

rock: is not his word_____ like a____ fire, and like a
- schlägt, und wie ein Ham - - - - mer, wie ein

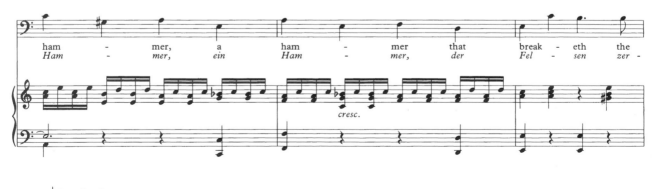

ham - mer, a ham - mer that break - eth the
Ham - mer, ein Ham - mer, der Fel - sen zer -

* ham - mer that   (Ewer)   † rock, like a   (Simrock, and uncorrected Ewer)   ** ham - mer that   (Ewer)

rock?   that break - eth the rock,   that break - eth the
- *schlägt,   der Fel - sen zer - schlägt,   zer - schlägt,*

rock; and like a fire,   like a ham - mer that
und wie ein Ham - mer, ein Ham - mer der

break - eth the rock;   is not his word   like a
Fel - sen zer - schlägt. Ist nicht sein Wort   wie ein

ham - mer that break - eth the rock, is not his
Ham - mer, der Fel - sen zer - schlägt. Ist nicht sein

word like a ham - mer that break - eth
Wort wie ein Ham - mer, der Fel - sen,

*  (Simrock and uncorrected Ewer)

break - eth the rock

No. 18

Air [Woe unto them]

Arioso

* Mendelssohn gives both notes, as alternatives.

No. 19   Recit. [O man of God, help thy people]
                     Recit. und Chor

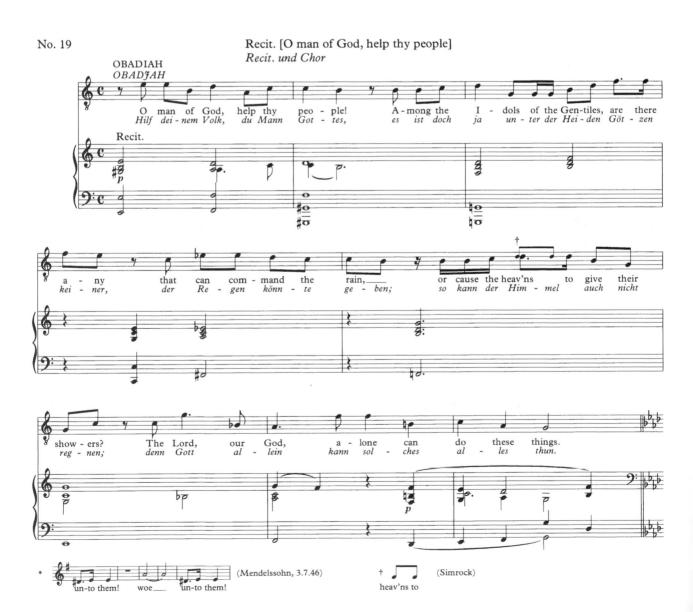

Recit. with Chorus [O Lord, thou hast overthrown]

*'Now look on us, etc.' (Mendelssohn 3.7.46) the dis- (Simrock)

ELIJAH
*ELIAS

Go up now child; and look to-ward the sea.
Ge-he hin-auf, Kna - be, und shau-e zum Mee-re zu,

Hath my pray - er been heard by the
ob der Herr mein Ge - bet er-

Recit.
THE YOUTH
DER KNABE (Soprano Solo)

Lord?   There is no - thing. The heav'ns are as brass, they are as brass a-
-hört.   Ich se - he nichts; der Him - mel ist e - hern ü - ber mei-nem

ELIJAH A
ELIAS   Tempo

- bove me. When the hea - vens are clo - sed up, be - cause they have sin - ned,
Haup - te. Wenn der Him - mel ver-schlos - sen wird, weil sie an dir

Tempo

___ have sin-ned a-gainst Thee; Yet, if they pray and con - fess, con-fess thy name,___ and
___ ge-sün-di-get ha - ben, und sie wer-den be - ten und dei - nen Na-men be-ken - nen

turn___ from their sin   when Thou dost af - flict them: Then hear from heav'n, and for -
und sich von ih - ren Sün-den be-keh - ren, so wol - lest du ih - nen

* ♩ 𝄾 ♪ ♩ ♪♪ (Mendelssohn, 3.7.46) † ♪ ♩ ♩ ♩ ♩ ♩ (Mendelssohn, 3.7.46) ** 𝄢 ♪ ♩ (Simrock)
Go up now   be-cause they have sinn'd,___ have   and turn

*Tenor and Bass: (Simrock)   † (Mendelssohn, 3.7.46)   **deep. (Simrock)   †† See Preface
sin: Help, send thy
sin: Help, send thy   Go up a-gain

* ♪ ♩ ♩| ♩   (Mendelssohn, 3.7.46)   *Tenor: Thanks be to God for all his mer - cies,___ for all his   (Ewer)

like a man's hand!

No. 20   Chorus [Thanks be to God]
Chor

*Bass: ♩ ♩ ♩ (Simrock)
    land, the

100

*Alto: (Simrock)
Thanks be to

†Tenor: (Simrock)
the thirs - ty land.

*Soprano: ♩ ⸿ | (Simrock)
God,

END OF PART THE FIRST   *ENDE DES ERSTEN THEILS*

SECOND PART [*ZWEITER THEIL*]

No. 21

Aria [Hear ye, Israel]
Aria

hear what the Lord_ speak - eth: 'Oh, hadst thou heed - ed, heed-ed my___ com -
hö - re des Herrn_ Stim - me! Ach dass du merk - test___ auf sein___ Ge -

- mand - ments! Oh, hadst thou heed - ed, oh, hadst thou heed-ed my com -
- bot! ach, dass du merk - test, merk - test___ auf sein Ge -

- mand-ments!' Hear ye, Is - ra-el! Is - ra-el!
- bot! Hö - re I - sra-el! I - sra-el!

piú adagio **Recitative**

hear_____ what the Lord_ speak - eth! Thus saith the Lord,___ the Re-deem-er of Is-ra-el
hö - re des Herrn_ Stim - me! So spricht der Herr, der Er - lö - ser I - sra-els,

Recitative

and his Ho - ly One, to him op-press-ed by ty - rants; thus saith the Lord:
sein Hei - li - ger zum Knecht der un-ter den Ty - ran-nen ist; so spricht der Herr:

*♩ ♪ (Ewer)   †See Preface for comment on this Recit.
- mand - ments

Tempo
Allegro maestoso ♩ = 132

'I, I am He that com - fort - eth; be not a-fraid, be not a-fraid,___ for
Ich, ich bin eu - er Trös - ter. Wei-che nicht, wei-che nicht, denn

I am thy God. I, I am He that com - fort - eth; be not a-
ich bin dein Gott! Ich, ich bin eu - er Trös - ter. Wei-che

- fraid, be not a-fraid, for___ I am thy___ God, I will strength - en___
nicht, wei - che nicht, denn___ ich bin dein___ Gott; ich stär - ke___

thee, I,_____ the Lord, will strength-en thee,
dich; wei_____ che nicht, ich stär - ke dich,

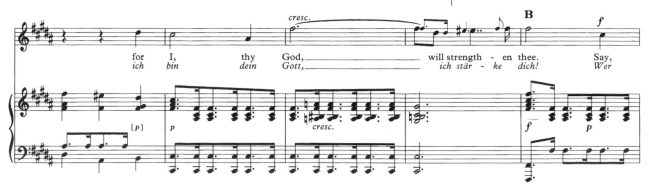

for I, thy God,_____ will strength - en thee. Say,
ich bin dein Gott,_____ ich stär - ke dich! Wer

B

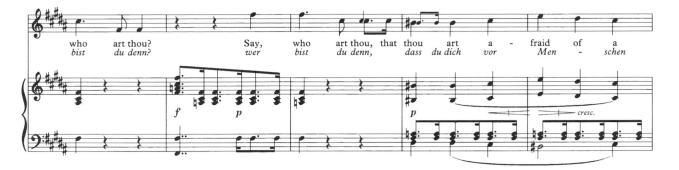

who art thou? Say, who art thou, that thou art a - fraid of a
bist du denn? *wer bist du denn,* *dass du dich vor Men - schen*

man that shall die; and for - get - test the Lord, the
fürch - test, die doch ster - ben? *und ver - gis - sest des Herrn,*

Lord thy Ma - ker, who hath stretch - ed forth the hea -
der dich ge - macht hat, *der den Him - mel aus - brei -*

- vens, and laid the earth's foun - da - tions, the earth's foun -
- tet, *und die Er - de grün - det,* *die Er - de*

- da - tions? Say, who art thou? I, I am He that
grün - det. *Wer bist du denn?* *Ich, ich bin eu - er*

114

No. 22

Chorus [Be not afraid]

Chor

Allegro maestoso, ma moderato ♩ = 112

SOPRANO *f*

Be not a - fraid, saith God the Lord. Be not a - fraid; thy help is
Fürch - te dich nicht, spricht un - ser Gott, fürch - te dich nicht, ich bin mit

ALTO *f*

Be not a - fraid, saith God the Lord. Be not a - fraid; thy help is
Fürch - te dich nicht, spricht un - ser Gott, fürch - te dich nicht, ich bin mit

TENOR *f*

Be not a - fraid, saith God the Lord. Be not a - fraid; thy help is
Fürch - te dich nicht, spricht un - ser Gott, fürch - te dich nicht, ich bin mit

BASS *f*

Be not a - fraid, saith God the Lord. Be not a - fraid; thy help is
Fürch - te dich nicht, spricht un - ser Gott, fürch - te dich nicht, ich bin mit

Allegro maestoso, ma moderato ♩ = 112

sf *ff* [*f*]

Ped.

near. Be not a - fraid, be not a -
dir. Fürch - te dich nicht, fürch - te dich

near. Be not a - fraid; thy help is near. Be not a -
dir. Fürch - te dich nicht, ich bin mit dir. Fürch - te dich

near. Be not a - fraid; thy help is near, help,_____ thy help is
dir. Fürch - te dich nicht, ich bin mit dir, ich,_____ ich bin mit

near. Be not a - fraid,_____ be not a -
dir. Fürch - te dich nicht,_____ fürch - te dich

- fraid; thy help is near, thy help is near, thy help is near.
nicht, ich bin mit dir, ich bin mit dir, ich bin mit dir.

- fraid; thy help is near, thy help is near, thy help is near, thy
nicht, ich bin mit dir, ich bin mit dir, ich bin mit dir, ich

near, thy help, thy help is near, thy help is near,
dir, mit dir, ich bin mit dir, ich bin mit dir,

- fraid; thy help is near, thy help is near, thy help is near, thy help is
nicht, ich bin mit dir, ich bin mit dir, ich bin mit dir, ich hel - fe

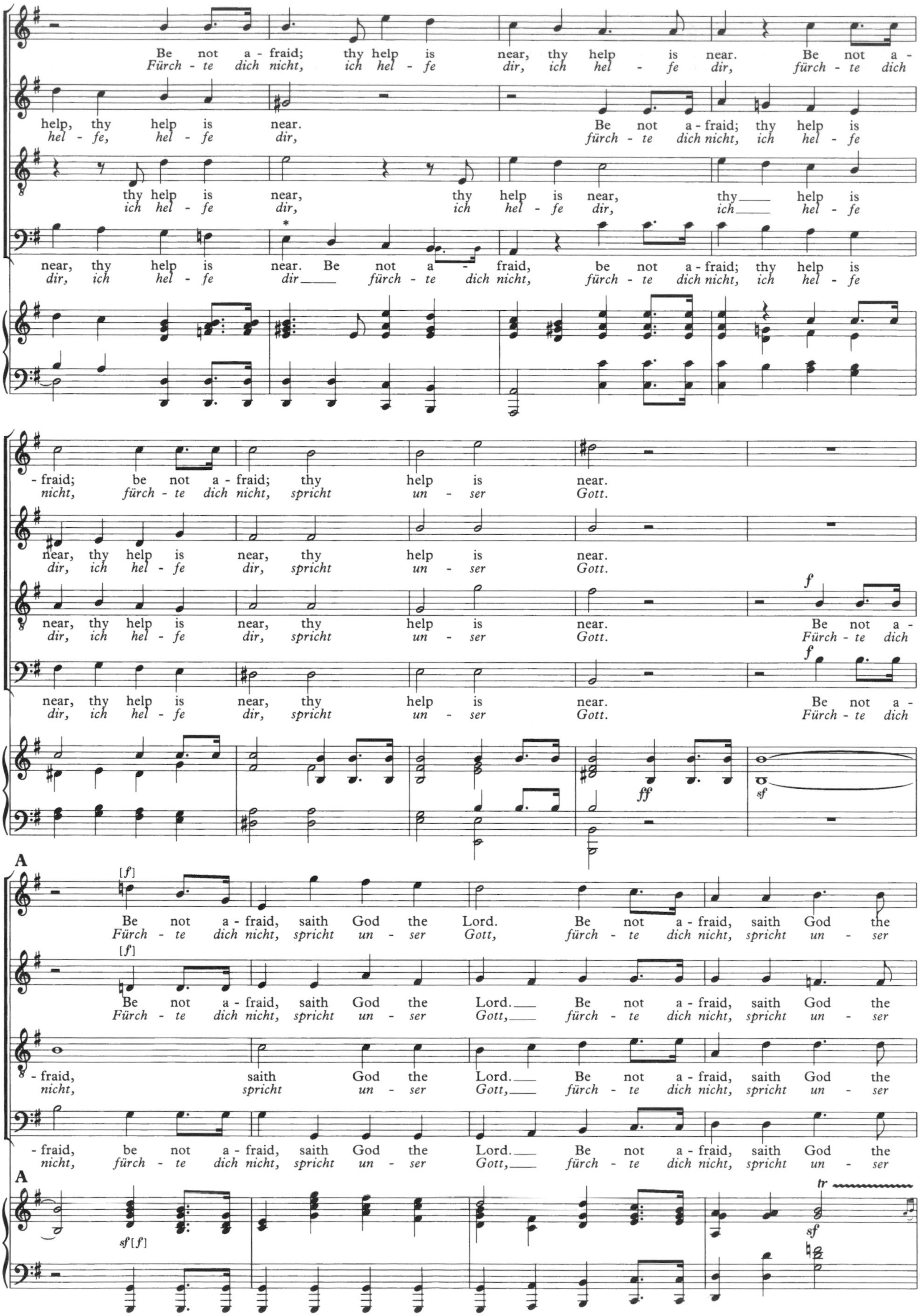

* Bass: (Simrock)
near._ Be not a-fraid,

Lord: thy help is near, thy help is near. God, the Lord thy
Gott, ich hel - fe dir, ich hel - fe dir, denn ich bin der
Lord: thy help is near, thy help is near. God, the Lord thy
Gott, ich hel - fe dir, ich hel - fe dir, denn ich bin der
Lord: thy help is near, thy help is near. God, the Lord thy
Gott, ich hel - fe dir, ich hel - fe dir, denn ich bin der
Lord: thy help is near, thy help is near. God, the Lord thy
Gott, ich hel - fe dir, ich hel - fe dir, denn ich bin der
tr
[sf]
Più animato ♩ = 138
God, say - eth un - to thee, 'Be not a - fraid!'
Herr dein Gott, der zu dir spricht: Fürch - te dich nicht!
God, say - eth un - to thee, 'Be not a - fraid!'
Herr dein Gott, der zu dir spricht: Fürch - te dich nicht!
God, say - eth un - to thee, 'Be not a - fraid!'
Herr dein Gott, der zu dir spricht: Fürch - te dich nicht!
God, say - eth un - to thee, 'Be not a - fraid!'
Herr dein Gott, der zu dir spricht: Fürch - te dich nicht!
Più animato ♩ = 138
f
sf
f
Though thou - sands lan - guish and fall be - side thee, and tens of thou - sands a - round thee
Ob tau - send fal - len zu dei - ner Sei - te und ze - hen - tau - send zu dei - ner
sf
simili

122

No. 23   Recitative and chorus [The Lord hath exalted thee]
                 Recitativo und Chor

* ♩ ♫ (Simrock)

smite_ all

126

* ♩ ♩ (Simrock)

gods do

* ♩ ♪ (Simrock)

brook of

No. 24   Chorus [Woe to him!]

Chor

Allegro Moderato ♩ = 100

SOPRANO

ALTO

TENOR

BASS

Woe to him!
We - he ihm!

Woe to him!
We - he ihm!

Woe to him!
We - he ihm!

Woe to him!
We - he ihm!

Allegro Moderato ♩ = 100

woe to him, he shall pe - rish; he clos - ed the hea-vens, he clos - ed the
we - he ihm! er muss ster - ben! War - um darf er den Him-mel, den Him - mel ver -

he shall pe - rish; he clos - ed the hea-vens, he clos - ed the
er muss ster - ben! War - um darf er den Him-mel, den Him - mel ver -

woe to him, he shall pe - rish; he clos - ed the hea-vens, he clos - ed the
we - he ihm! er muss ster - ben! War - um darf er den Him-mel, den Him - mel ver -

woe to him, he shall pe - rish; he clos - ed the hea-vens, he clos - ed the
we - he ihm! er muss ster - ben! War - um darf er den Him-mel, den Him - mel ver -

hea - vens! And why hath he spo - ken in the name of the Lord? and why hath he
- schlies-sen? wa - rum darf er weis - sa - gen im Na - men des Herrn? wa - rum darf er

hea - vens! And why hath he spo - ken in the name of the Lord? and why hath he
- schlies-sen? wa - rum darf er weis - sa - gen im Na - men des Herrn? wa - rum darf er

hea - vens! And why hath he spo - ken in the name of the Lord? and why hath he
- schlies-sen? wa - rum darf er weis - sa - gen im Na - men des Herrn? wa - rum darf er

hea - vens! And why hath he spo - ken in the name of the Lord? and why hath he
- schlies-sen? wa - rum darf er weis - sa - gen im Na - men des Herrn? wa - rum darf er

All voices: pe - rish, shall pe - rish; for he clos-ed,   (Simrock)

spo - ken in the name_ of the Lord? and why, and why hath he thus
weis - sa - gen im Na - men des Herrn? wa - rum? wa - rum darf er weis -
spo - ken in the name_ of the Lord? and why, and why,
weis - sa - gen im Na - men des Herrn? wa - rum? wa - rum?
spo - ken in the name_ of the Lord? and why, and why,
weis - sa - gen im Na - men des Herrn? wa - rum? wa - rum?
spo - ken in the name of the Lord? and why, and why, why hath he clo - sed the
weis - sa - gen im Na - men des Herrn? wa - rum? wa - rum darf er den Him - mel ver -
spo - ken, and why, and why hath he
- sa - gen? wa - rum? wa - rum darf er
and why hath he spo - ken in the name of the
wa - rum darf er weis - sa - gen im Na - men des
sf
and why hath he spo - ken in the name of the Lord, the name_ of the Lord? and
wa - rum darf er weis - sa - gen im Na - men des Herrn, in Na - men des Herrn? wa -
hea - vens? and why, and why, and why,
- schlies - sen? wa - rum? wa - rum? wa - rum?
sf sf [sf] sf sf [sf] [sf] sf sf sf
spo - ken in the name of the Lord? and why hath he spo - ken in the name of the
weis - sa - gen im Na - men des Herrn? wa - rum darf er weis - sa - gen im Na - men des
Lord, the name of the Lord? and why, and why, and why hath he
Herrn, im Na - men des Herrn? wa - rum? wa - rum? wa - rum darf er
why, and why hath he thus spo - ken, and why hath he
- rum, wa - rum darf er weis - sa - gen? wa - rum darf er
and why hath he spo - ken in the name of the Lord, the name of the
wa - rum darf er weis - sa - gen in Na - men des Herrn, in Na - men des
[sf] [sf] [sf] [sf] [sf] [sf] sf sf [sf]

134

*Bass: ♩. ♪ (Simrock)
pe - rish

No. 25

Recit. [Man of God]
Recitativo

* ♩♪ (Simrock)

words be

Lord thy God doth go, doth go with thee:___ He will not fail thee, He
Herr dein Gott wird sel - ber mit dir wan - deln, er___ wird die Hand nicht ab -

___ will not for - sake thee. Now be - gone, be - gone, and bless me; now___ be -
- thun noch dich ver-las - sen. Zie - he hin___ und seg - ne uns auch! zie - he hin___ be -

ELIJAH
ELIAS

- gone, and bless me___ al - so. Though strick - en___ they have not griev-ed! Tar-ry
und seg - ne uns auch! Sie wol - len___ sich nicht be - keh - ren! Blei-be

here my ser-vant, the Lord be with thee. I jour-ney hence to the wil - der-ness.
hier du Kna-be, der Herr sei mit euch! Ich ge - he hin in die Wüs - te.

attacca No.26

*See Preface for this 4–bar phrase.

No. 26

Aria [It is enough]

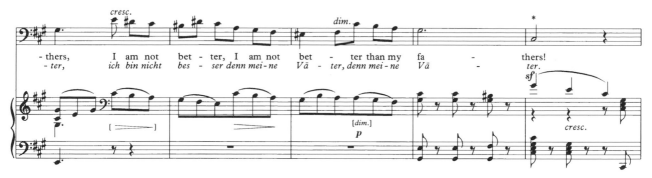

* 𝅘𝅥 𝄾 𝄾 (Ewer)
−thers!

† 𝅘𝅥 𝅘𝅥 𝅘𝅥 (Ewer)
va‑ni‑ty

for the Lord God of Hosts, ve-ry jea-lous for the
um den Gott Ze - be - oth, ge - ei - fert um den

Lord, the_ Lord God of Hosts, and I, e - ven I on - ly am left;___
Herrn, den_ Gott_ Ze - ba - oth. Und ich bin al - lein ü - brig ge - blie - ben;

and they seek my life, and they seek my life to take
und sie steh'n da - nach dass sie mir mein Le ben neh -

it, to take it a - way!___
- men, mein Le ben neh - - men!___

Adagio ♩ = 66

It is e - nough, it is e - nough!
Es ist ge - nug, es ist ge - nug!

Adagio ♩ = 66

*Small notes as printed in Ewer and Simrock VS.   † (Simrock)

the Lord_

It is e-nough, O Lord, now take a-way my life,___ for I am not
Es ist ge-nug, so nimm nun Herr_ mei-ne See_ le, ich bin nicht

bet-ter than my fa___thers! Now let me die,
bes-ser denn mei-ne Vä___ter. Nimm nun o Herr,

Lord,_____ take a-way_ my life!
nimm,_____ nimm o Herr mei-ne See-le!

No. 27   Recit. [See, now he sleepeth]
                          Recitativo

TENOR

See, now_ he sleep-eth be-neath a ju-ni-per tree in the wil-der-ness! and there the
Sie-he,_ er schläft_ un-ter dem Wach-hol-der, in der Wüs_ te; a-ber die

*an-gels of the Lord en-camp_ round a-bout all them that fear Him.
En-gel des Herrn la-gern sich um die her, so ihn fürch-ten.

*'angel – – – encampeth' (Simrock) but see Preface   †   (Simrock)

No. 28

Terzetto [Lift thine eyes] [The Angels]

Terzetto [Die Engel]

*Alto: ♩ ♩ (Ewer)
com-eth

† ♫ ♫ (Ewer)
from the

** Sop.2 (Ewer)
Lord, the Ma - ker

attacca No. 29

No. 29   Chorus [He, watching over Israel]
                        Chor

*Tenor: (Ewer) slum -

No. 30

Recit. [Arise, Elijah]
Recitativo

* strength for naught,— and in vain! (Simrock)

† Thou wouldst rend the hea-vens, (Simrock)

* strength, have spent my strength for naught (Ewer 1852)

152

No. 31 THE ANGEL (Alto)
DER ENGEL

Aria [O rest in the Lord]
Aria

O rest in the Lord, wait pa - tient - ly for Him, and He shall give thee thy heart's de - sires: O rest in the Lord, wait pa - tient - ly for Him, and He shall give thee thy heart's de - sires, and He shall give thee thy heart's de - sires. *Com - mit thy way un - to Him, and trust in Him; com - mit thy way un - to Him, and trust in Him, and fret not thy -

Sei stil - le dem Herrn, und war - te auf ihn; der wird dir ge - ben was dein Herz wünscht; sei stil - le dem Herrn, und war - te auf ihn; der wird dir ge - ben was dein Herz wünscht; der wird dir ge - ben was dein Herz wünscht. Be - fiehl ihm dei - ne We - ge und hof - fe auf ihn; be - fiehl ihm dei - ne We - ge und hof - fe auf ihn. Steh' ab vom

*See Preface for Mendelssohn's comment on the words.

† ♩ ♪ (Simrock)

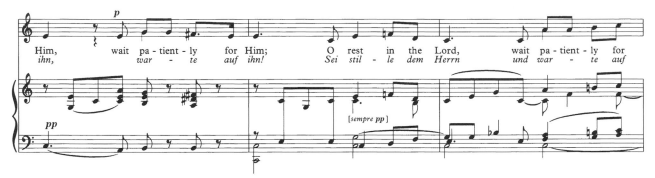

No. 32   Chorus [He that shall endure to the end]
Chor

*Sop: (Simrock)
He that

†Small notes not in Ewer or Simrock VS.

No. 33

Recit. [Night falleth round me]
Recitativo

*Mendelssohn's MM list of April 1847 gives ♩ = 76, followed by Ewer.

** All sources put piano fermatas over the preceding minim rests.

† ♩♩ and (Simrock)

†† letter 2.2.47 includes

No. 34   Chorus [Behold, God the Lord passed by!]
                                 Chor

*See Preface for Mendelssohn's varying proposals for English rhythms in this number.

160

162

E
fire, but yet the Lord was not in the fire. And af - ter the
Feu - er, a - ber der Herr war nicht im Feu - er. Und nach dem
fire, there came a still small voice:
Feu - er kam ein stil - les, sanf - tes Sau - sen.
And in that
Und in dem
sempre pp

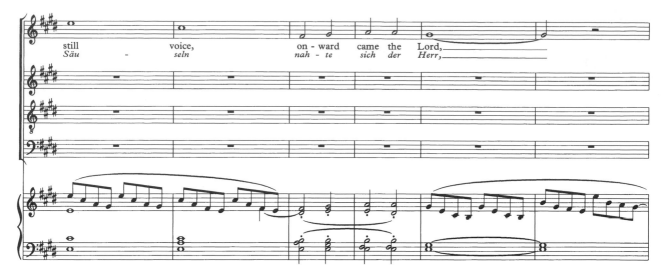

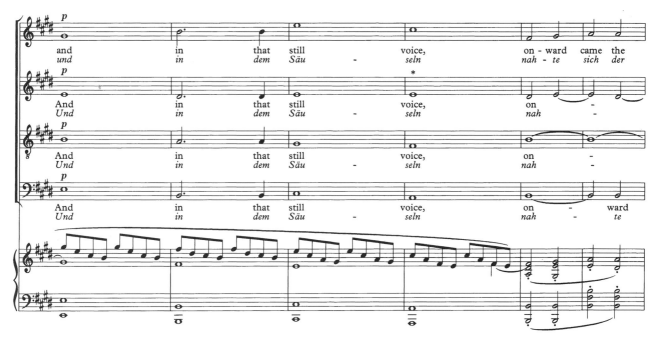

*Alto: (Ewer)
voice,___ on___

No. 35   Recit., Quartet, and Chorus [Holy, holy, holy]

Recitativo

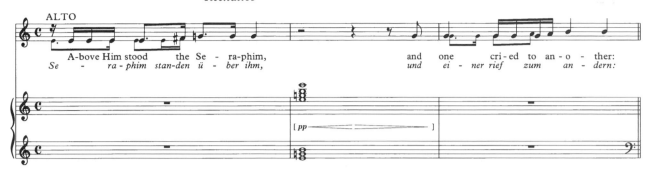

Quartett mit Chor

*The small notes are from the orchestral score only. †Piano: (Ewer and Simrock VS)

*Alto1 solo: (Simrock)
earth

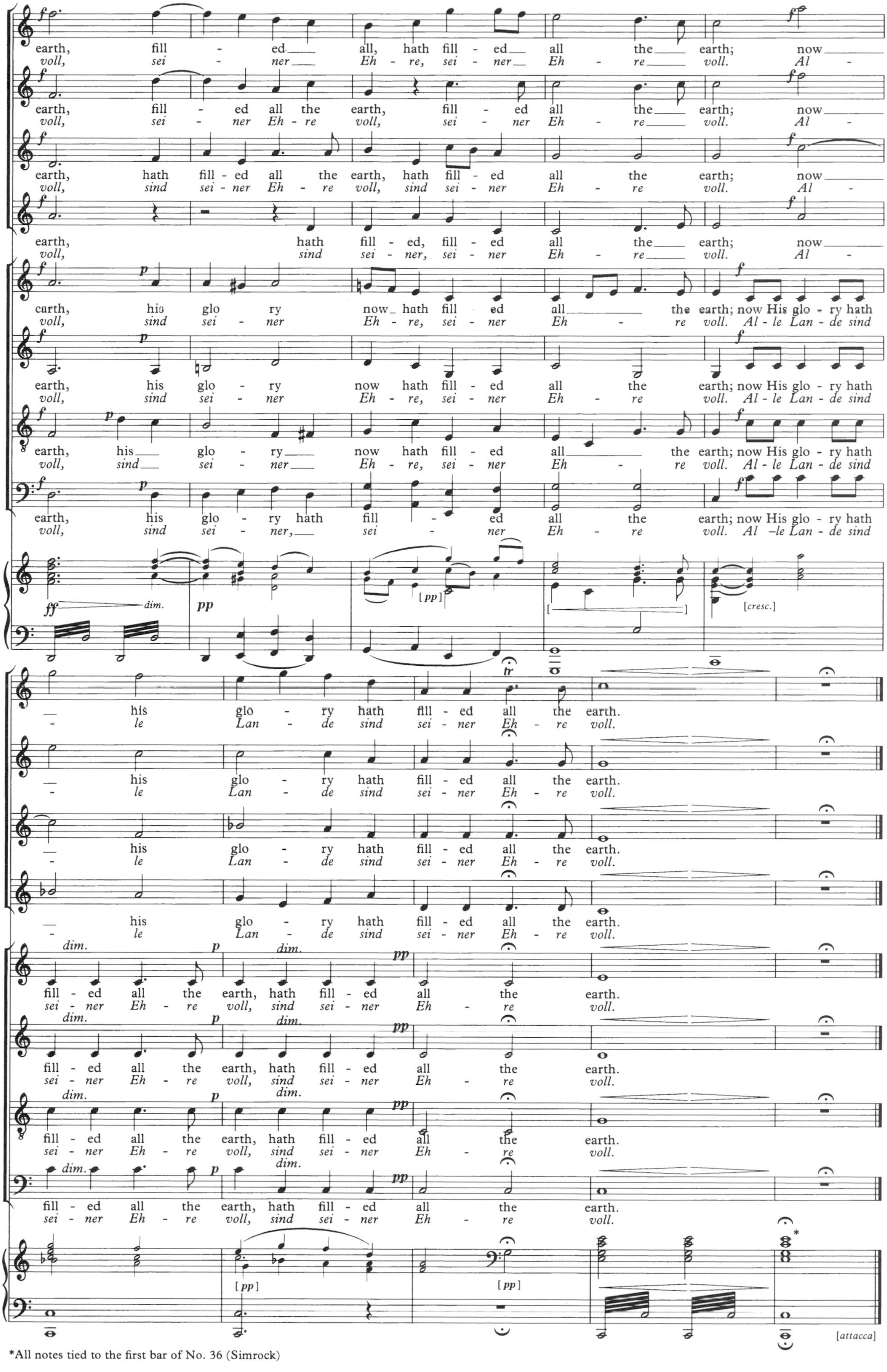

*All notes tied to the first bar of No. 36 (Simrock)

No. 36

Recit: Chorus [Go, return upon thy way!]
Chor Recitativo

*Tenor and Bass: (Simrock) — Go, return

†Sop. and Alto: etc.(Simrock) — Go re-turn

**go thy way; (Simrock)

[I go on my way in the strength of the Lord]

ELIJAH
ELIAS

Più mosso ♩ = 84

I go on my
Ich ge - he hin -

way in the strength____ of the Lord.
- ab in der Kraft____ des Herrn!

[Recit.]

For Thou art my
du bist ja der

Lord, and I will suf - fer for Thy sake.____ My heart is there - fore
Herr! ich muss um dei - net wil - len lei - den, da - rum freu - et sich mein

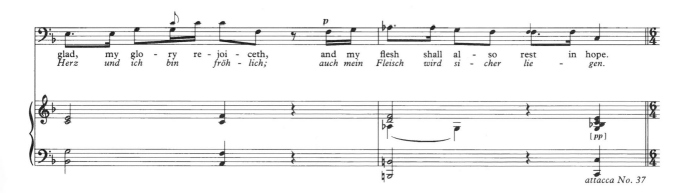

glad, my glo - ry re - joi - ceth, and my flesh shall al - so rest in hope.
Herz und ich bin fröh - lich; auch mein Fleisch wird si - cher lie - gen.

attacca No. 37

No. 37   Arioso [For the mountains shall depart]

* (Simrock)

kind - ness shall not, shall

peace,_____ of thy peace_____ be re - mov - ed, nei - ther shall_____ the
fal - len, und der Bund er soll nicht fal - len, und der Bund dei - nes

co - ve-nant of thy peace_____ be re - mov - ed; but thy kind-ness shall not___ de -
Frie - dens, dei - nes Frie - dens soll___ nicht fal - len. Dei - ne Gna - de wird nicht von mir

-part,___ shall not ___ de - part, but thy kind - ness shall not___ de -
wei - chen, wird nicht von mir wei - chen! Dei - ne Gna - de wird nicht von mir

-part, shall not___ de - part from me; nei - ther shall be re -
wei - chen, nicht von mir wei - chen und der Bund_____ be re -

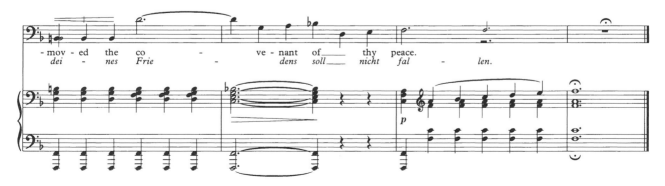

-mov - ed the co - ve-nant of___ thy peace.
dei - nes Frie - dens soll___ nicht fal - len.

Chorus [Then did Elijah]

Chor

*Bass: (Ewer only) whirl-wind

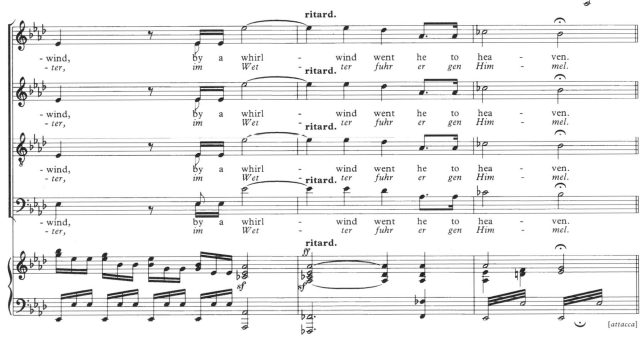

[attacca]

No. 39
TENOR

Aria [Then shall the righteous shine forth]

*Ewer 1852 gives *Andante* for voice and *Andante sostenuto* for piano(!)

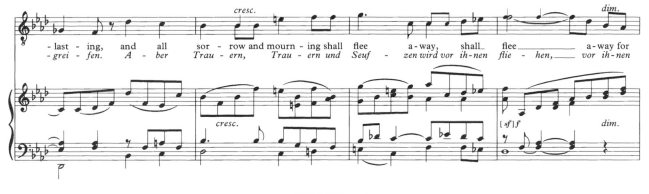

-last - ing, and all sor - row and mourn-ing shall flee a-way, shall flee____ a-way for
-grei - fen. A - ber Trau - ern, Trau-ern und Seuf - zen wird vor ih-nen flie - hen,____ vor ih-nen

ev - er. Then, then__ shall the right-eous shine forth as the sun in their heav'n-ly
flie - hen. Dann wer-den die Ge-rech-ten leuch - ten, wie die Son - ne in ih - res

Fa - ther's realm, shine forth, shine in their heav'n - ly Fa - ther's realm,
Va - ters Reich. Leuch - ten, leuch - ten in ih - res Va - ters__ Reich.

shine forth as the sun____ in their heav'n-ly Fa - ther's realm, then
Leuch - ten wie die Son - ne in ih - res Va - ters__ Reich, in

shall the right - eous shine in their heav'n-ly Fa - ther's realm.
ih - res Va - ters Reich, in ih - res Va - ters Reich.

*No pause in Ewer, but added in Ewer 1852.

No. 40   Recit. and Chorus [Behold, God hath sent Elijah]

*This ossia part is as given in Ewer 1852 and Simrock. The full size (English) version is from Ewer 1847.

[No. 41]

Chorus [But the Lord]
Chor

*All voices: ♩ ♩ ♩. ♪ (Ewer 1847, and implied by underlay in Simrock, though no separate notes are printed; Ewer 1852 follows main text.) ;
ris-ing on his

♩ ♩. ♪♩♩♩♩. ♪♩ ♩ ♩.   (Mendelssohn, 26.9.46). See also Preface.   †See Preface for comments on the
And from the ris-ing he shall call his   name.   tempo of this section.

*See Preface for Mendelssohn's comment on words.

*Piano, R.H. Ewer and Simrock VS have Cs instead of Ds on second beat.

†Mendelssohn 26.9.46: "I prefer  "
He shall call___ up - on his name, etc.

attacca Quartetto

No. 41

Quartetto [O come every one that thirsteth]

*Ewer adds a bass to this chord:

*Ten: (Ewer)   †Sop: (Simrock)

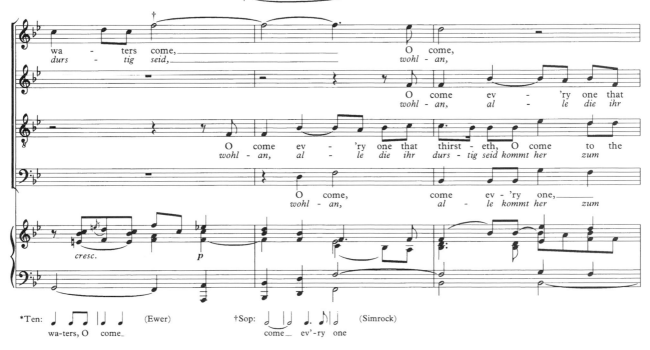

*Ten: (Ewer)
wa-ters, O come

†Sop: (Simrock)
come ev'-ry one

*Sop: (Ewer) come ev-'ry

†Piano: (Ewer and Simrock VS)

No. 42   Chorus [And then shall your light break forth]

*Schluss–Chor

*See Preface for Mendelssohn's comment on this heading.

name is in all the na - tions, Lord how ex - cel - lent
Na - me in al - len Lan - den! Herr wie herr - lich
na - tions, in all the na - tions, in all the na - tions,
Lan - den, in al - len Lan - den, in al - len Lan - den,
Lord our Cre - a - tor, how
Herr un - ser Herr - scher, wie
f
in all the na - tions, in all the na - tions,
in al - len Lan - den, in al - len Lan - den,
all the na - tions, Lord our Cre - a - tor, how
al - len Lan - den! Herr un - ser Herr - scher, wie
Lord our Cre - a - tor, how
Herr un - ser Herr - scher, wie
ex - cel - lent thy name is in all the na - tions, in all
herr - lich ist dein Na - me in al - len Lan - den, in al -
in all the na - tions, how ex - cel - lent in
in al - len Lan - den! wie herr - lich in al - len
ex - cel - lent thy name is,
herr - lich ist dein Na - me,
ex - cel - lent thy name is in all the na - tions, in all the
herr - lich ist dein Na - me in al - len Lan - den! in al - len
the na - tions, in all the na - tions!
- len Lan - den, in al - len Lan - den!

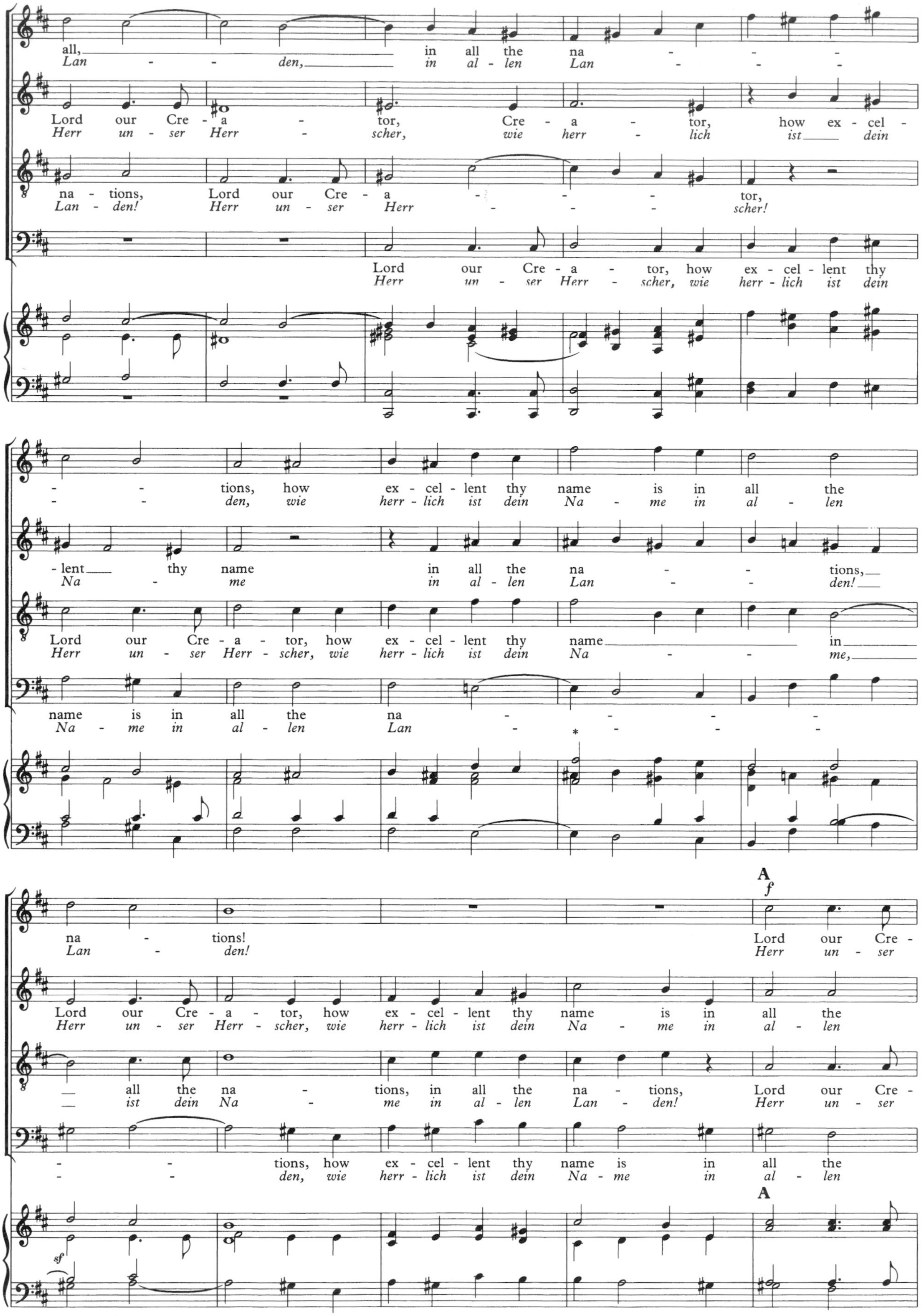

*Piano: 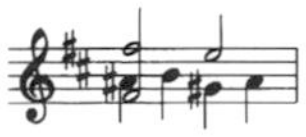 (Ewer and Simrock VS)

*Sop: (Simrock; clearly a misprint – in full score the instruments have e″, d″)

-a - tor, Lord, Lord our Cre - a - tor, how ex - cel - lent thy name is
Herr - scher, Herr, Herr un - ser Herr - scher, wie herr - lich ist dein Na - me

- lent thy name is, Lord our Cre - a - tor, how ex - cel - lent thy name is
ist dein Na - me! Herr un - ser Herr - scher, wie herr - lich ist dein Na - me

- tor, Lord our Cre - a - tor, how ex - cel - lent thy name is
scher, Herr un - ser Herr - scher, wie herr - lich ist dein Na - me

-a - tor, Lord our Cre - a - tor, how ex - cel - lent thy name is
herr - lich, Herr un - ser Herr - scher, wie herr - lich ist dein Na - me

in all the na - tions, in all the na - tions! Thou fill - est
in al - len Lan - den, in al - len Lan - den, da man dir

in all the na - tions, in all the na - tions! Thou fill - est
in al - len Lan - den, in al - len Lan - den, da man dir

in all the na - tions, in all the na - tions! Thou fill - est
in al - len Lan - den, in al - len Lan - den, da man dir

in all the na - tions, in all the na - tions! Thou fill - est
in al - len Lan - den, in al - len Lan - den, da man dir

heav'n with glo - ry. Lord our Cre -
dank't im Him - mel. Herr un - ser

heav'n with thy glo - ry. Lord our Cre -
dan - ket im Him - mel. Herr un - ser

heav'n with thy glo - ry. Lord our Cre - a - tor, our Cre -
dan - ket im Him - mel. Herr un - ser Herr - scher! un - ser

heav'n with thy glo - ry. Lord our Cre - a - tor, Lord, our Cre -
dan - ket im Him - mel. Herr un - ser Herr - scher! Herr un - ser

Printed and bound in Great Britain by
Caligraving Limited Thetford Norfolk

FINE